We hope you enjoy this book. Please return or renew it by the due date. You can renew it at **www.norfolk.gov.uk/libraries** or by using our free library app. Otherwise you can phone **0344 800 8020** - please have your library card and PIN ready. You can sign up for email reminders too.

First published in 2017 by
The Crowood Press Ltd
Ramsbury, Marlborough
Wiltshire SN8 2HR

www.crowood.com

British Library Cataloguing-in-Publication Data
A catalogue record for this book is available from the British Library.

ISBN 978 1 78500 302 8

Mapping in this book is sourced from the following products: OS Explorer 133, 134, 145, 146,
160 and 161
© Crown copyright 2016 Ordnance Survey. Licence number 100038003

Every effort has been made to ensure the accuracy of this book. However, changes can occur
during the lifetime of an edition. The Publishers cannot be held responsible for any errors or
omissions or for the consequences of any reliance on the information given in this book, but
should be very grateful if walkers could let us know of any inaccuracies by writing to us at
the address above or via the website.

As with any outdoor activity, accidents and injury can occur. We strongly advise readers to
check the local weather forecast before setting out and to take an OS map. The Publishers
accept no responsibility for any injuries which may occur in relation to following the walk
descriptions contained within this book.

Typeset by Jean Cussons Typesetting, Diss, Norfolk
Printed and bound in Malaysia by Times Offset (M) Sdn Bhd

Contents

How to Use this Book

The walks in the book are ordered by distance, starting with the shortest. An information panel for each walk shows the distance, start point, a summary of route terrain and level of difficulty (Easy/Moderate/Difficult), OS map(s) required, and suggested pubs/cafés at the start/end of walk or *en route*.

Maps

There are 84 maps covering the 100 walks. Some of the walks are extensions of existing routes and the information panel for these walks will tell you the distance of the short and long versions of the walk. For those not wishing to undertake the longer versions of these walks, the 'short-cuts' are shown on the map in red.

The routes marked on the maps are punctuated by a series of numbered waypoints. These relate to the same numbers shown in the walk description.

Start Points

The start of each walk is given as a postcode and also a six-figure grid reference number prefixed by two letters (which indicates the relevant square on the National Grid). More information on grid references is found on Ordnance Survey maps.

Parking

Many of the car parks suggested are public, but for some walks you will have to park on the roadside or in a lay-by. Please be considerate when leaving your car and do not block access roads or gates. Also, if parking in a pub car park for the duration of the walk, please try to avoid busy times.

Countryside Code

- Consider the local community and other people enjoying the outdoors
- Leave gates and property as you find them and follow paths
- Leave no trace of your visit and take litter home
- Keep dogs under effective control
- Plan ahead and be prepared
- Follow advice and local signs

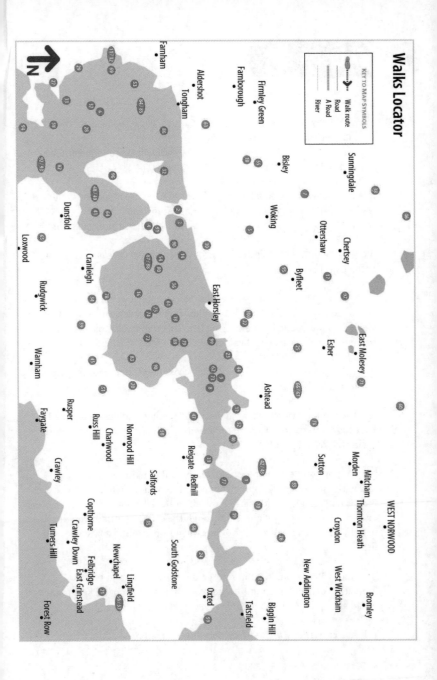

Walks Locator

KEY TO MAP SYMBOLS

Walk route
Road
A Road
River

Chipstead

Start At TQ278567, the recreation ground car park, CR5 3SE

Distance 2¾ miles (4.5km)

Summary An easy but undulating walk through fields and woodland trails

Parking Plenty available at the start

Maps OS Sheets Landranger 187; Explorer 146

Where to eat and drink The White Hart, Chipstead www.white-hart-chipstead.co.uk

Big views of the surrounding countryside are enjoyed on this walk through a secluded valley.

1 From the car park walk along High Road, going away from the crossroads to reach the White Hart pub. There, fork left and after a few yards take the public footpath going left. This track leads to a barrier beyond which it descends. Bear left to reach a road (Castle Road).

2 Cross, go through a gate and head across the field to another gate in the hedgerow opposite.

3 Descend to reach the fenced electricity compound beside the road. Here look over to your right to see Rumbolds Castle Cottage, the house beside the railway viaduct.

4 Do not use the gate onto the road, instead remaining in the field and with the electricity compound in front of you, turn left to follow the perimeter of the field uphill to reach a gate, keeping the bushes and wire fence to your right. Go through the gate and walk through a narrow belt of trees. Beyond the trees, turn right around a large sloping field.

5 About 50yd along the top side, go up through a gap to reach a footpath. Turn left along this broad path. Stay with the path, keeping ahead at a path crossing and bearing right at a later fork.

6 At a crossroads with a green Self-guided Trail marker post, turn

left. Descend and pass through a gate, go through the field to reach another gate.

7 Here, keep to the left and follow the Permissive Footpath with the 'Shabdon and Upper Gatton circular walk' marker post.

8 At the gate at the top of the hill, turn left to follow the public footpath straight across the field to reach a gate and a chalky track.

9 Bear left onto the track; you are now walking parallel to the outwards route, but on the other side of the valley.

10 When another gate is reached, turn right to reach a road (Castle Road again).

11 Do not go out onto the road, instead turn right, staying inside the field going uphill to reach its top where you emerge close to the village pumphouse of Chipstead. Turn left to reach the pond and the start of the walk.

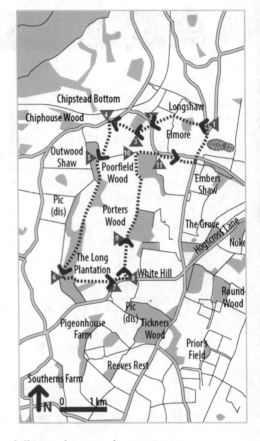

Points of interest

Rumbolds Castle Cottage – Next to the Tattenham Corner railway bridge is a 16th Century Grade II listed, timber framed cottage. It was, until the early 1900s, an inn.

Shalford and St Catherine's Chapel

Start At TQ000477, The Seahorse, Shalford GU4 8BU

Distance 2¾ miles (4.5km)

Summary An easy walk alongside the River Wey and part of the North Downs Way

Parking Plenty in nearby side streets or in the car park at The Seahorse

Maps OS Sheets Landranger 186; Explorer 145

Where to eat and drink The Seahorse, www.theseahorseguildford.co.uk. Open daily from 11:00 for drinks; food served from midday. Sunday opening 11:30. Choices include traditional favourites to freshly made pizzas and pastas. Moderately priced

An interesting walk along a stretch of the River Wey with an optional detour to visit a ruined Chapel.

1 Beyond the wall of The Seahorse car park, turn left along the bridleway. This bears left, passing the rear gardens of some houses and is signposted to Godalming.

2 After roughly 375yd, turn right, go through the gate and pass the 'Shalford Water Meadows' information board. Drop down to the water meadows of the River Wey. Keep ahead over the walkway and go along the bank to reach the Riff Raff weir.

3 Go around the cottage, cross to the other bank at the lock and continue along the towpath. You can just see St Catherine's Chapel jutting into the sky ahead. At the footbridge, you can either clamber up the very steep and sandy hill to have a look at the ruins, or instead use the lane a few yards further on by the stone seat and miniature bridge.

4 To continue the walk, go over the footbridge, turn left onto the North Downs Way and then turn right after a few yards and head away from the river.

⑤ Cross a playing field and, at the main road, continue ahead along Pilgrims Way.

⑥ At the bend opposite the Echo Pit Road nameboard, bear right following the North Downs Way fingerpost. Soon you will reach Chantry Cottage situated at the entrance to Chantry Woods.

⑦ Turn right onto the sandy footpath and follow it to reach a residential road. Turn left onto the road and keep ahead, use the footpath running alongside.

⑧ Cross the road at the bottom, go up the steps, over the stile and bear right and cross the field beyond. At the end of the field go through the metal gate and down the steps where very shortly you will reach Shalford Mill. Continue to the road to finish the walk at The Seahorse.

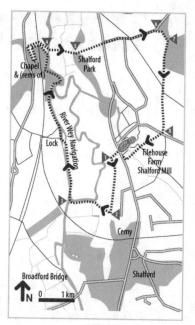

Points of interest

St Catherine's Chapel – The chapel, dating from the 14th century, is now a ruin. It lies on the route of the old Pilgrim's Way that ran from Winchester to Canterbury.

Chantry Cottage – The Chantries, or Chantry Woods, got their name from the chantry set up in 1486 by a man named Henry Norbridge. In the Middle Ages a chantry was an endowment, which paid for a priest to pray or sing for souls of the dead. The name derives from the French *chanter*, to sing.

Shalford Mill – The mill, which dates from the 18th century, sits astride the River Tillingbourne, a short distance from its confluence with the Wey. It was used as a corn mill until 1914. Having fallen into disrepair, it was restored in the early 1930s through the efforts of a group of enthusiasts known as Ferguson's Gang. The machinery is largely still intact. The building is now owned by the National Trust and is open to the public.

Chantry Woods and Pewley Down

START At TQ021484, Halfpenny Lane car park beside St Martha's Hill, GU4 8PZ

DISTANCE Distance 3 miles (4.75km)

SUMMARY A moderate walk due to a couple of steep ascents

PARKING Free parking at the start

MAPS OS Sheets Landranger 186; Explorer 145

WHERE TO EAT AND DRINK Provisions can be bought in nearby Albury or Chilworth; there are no refreshments stops en route

A pleasant walk along a couple of ridges with fine views and through shaded woodlands.

1️⃣ From the car park at the western foot of St Martha's Hill, walk left along Halfpenny Lane to find the North Downs Way on your right. Fork left immediately. The path rises through woodland to reach a campsite on the left. Just after this, go through a gate on the left and continue along the sandy path keeping the woods close by on your right. Continue past a bench commemorating a Golden Wedding Anniversary on your right, and enter the woodland.

2️⃣ This path initially descends, and then rises up using 35 steps. Beyond this, walk gently downhill eventually passing several benches and also catching a glimpse of Guildford Cathedral half-right. The main path now curls right to reach Chantry Cottage.

3️⃣ Make your way through to the car park. Here turn right, walking along the raised path above the car park to reach a road. Keep on the pavement and continue up to the left-hand sharp bend.

4️⃣ Then keep ahead up Northdown Lane with its substantial houses.

5️⃣ When the lane bears right at Eden House, take the raised path alongside the interesting brick wall. Ascend to the top of Pewley Down using the main chalky path.

6 At the top, by the green bench, turn right along the ridge going past the commemorative pedestal.

7 Then go down half-right by the hedgerow. Maintain this direction to the end of the fields going straight over a crossing track. Keep going until you reach a junction with two notice boards. Go straight ahead to enter the woods for a short ascent, which returns you to the road. Turn left to reach the car park where the walk started.

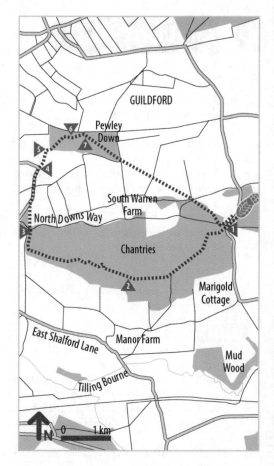

Points of interest

Guildford Cathedral – The Cathedral stands in a commanding spot on Stag Hill, so named because the Kings of England used to hunt here – overlooking the University of Surrey; its solid red brick outline is visible for miles around. Completed in 1961, it is immortalized in the 1976 film *The Omen*.

Chinthurst Hill

START At TQ017452, The Grantley Arms, Wonersh GU5 0PE

DISTANCE 3 miles (4.75km)

SUMMARY A moderate walk – easy when flat, more challenging on the ascent of Chinthurst Hill

PARKING On-street parking available in roads near the start

MAPS OS Sheets Landranger 186; Explorer 145

WHERE TO EAT AND DRINK The Grantley Arms, www.thegrantleyarms. webstarts.com/index.html. Food served daily from 12:00–14:30, 18:00–21:00; Tuesday and Wednesday till 21:30; Sunday all day till 21:00. Open daily from 12:00–21:00; Friday and Saturday 12:00–21:30

An interesting walk around the village of Wonersh with a climb up to a folly for a wonderful view.

① From the pub go along The Street towards Bramley, as indicated above the tile-covered seat shelter. Very soon the church tower comes into view. Just beyond the drive to Wonersh House (private), turn left through the archway, crossing the green to enter the churchyard of St John the Baptist up five steps. Bear right around the wall to return to the road. Cross the road and turn left, after 50yd go right along the footpath beyond the wall of Green Place using the metal kissing gate.

② Keep ahead through another gate, passing the bowling green to the right. The path joins a gravel drive, follow it to a road.

③ Cross the road and turn left. About 75yd past the junction with Blackheath Lane, turn right onto the drive of Little Tangley, then immediately bear left to take a footpath through a well hidden gap in the bushes.

④ Follow the iron fencing until the path joins a driveway which continues around a double bend towards a nursery.

⑤ Opposite the Old Coach House, turn left at a finger post. At this point, St Martha's Church is visible on top of the hill ahead just to the right.

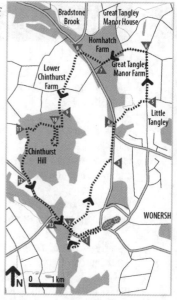

6 At the end of the field, there is a cluster of buildings around Great Tangley Manor. Turn left here, going along the Downs Link.

7 After about ¼ mile and shortly before the busy road, look out for a right turn. Take this, continuing on the Downs Link to reach the road.

8 Cross with care, and pass the side of the red-tile-roofed Falcon Cottage. At a junction, keep ahead, following a signpost to 'The Tower'.

9 The ascent under the trees is assisted by steps and zig-zags; there is even a seat placed at the crossing track on which to regain your breath before the final push to the summit! At the top, there is not only the tower, but a rewarding view and plenty of room to sit, relax and perhaps enjoy a picnic.

10 To continue the walk, return to the seat at the crossing. Now turn left along the track. Walk to a wooden barrier, where you join a private sweeping driveway.

11 Turn right and follow the bend to descend to a road.

12 Turn left here.

13 Keep ahead at the junction to return to Wonersh.

Points of interest

Tower – Standing at just less than 400ft, the tower on the top of Chinthurst Hill is an 18th century folly. The grassland around it provides an excellent picnic spot and a place to enjoy the beautiful view.

Send Church

Start At TQ018560, The New Inn, Send GU23 7EN

Distance 3 miles (4.75km)

Summary An easy, level riverside and water meadow walk

Parking Parking for patrons of the pub or in the nearby side street

Maps OS Sheets Landranger 186; Explorer 145

Where to eat and drink The New Inn, www.thenewinnsend.com. Casual and everyday style food made from fresh, locally sourced ingredients. Open daily from 12:00–21:00; Friday and Saturday 12:00–21:30

A pretty section of the River Wey and the Navigation Canal with a visit to Send Church.

Please note This walk is not recommended after prolonged rain due to the possibility of waterlogged ground. The watermeadow may be wet at any time so appropriate footwear is advisable.

1 The Wey Navigation runs beside the New Inn; follow the gravel drive beside it for 100yd, going south from the Inn, and cross a footbridge. Follow the path ahead to reach a drive and continue, to cross two branches of the river.

2 In front of Fisher's Farm, turn left over a stile and follow a track, passing some paddocks, to the entrance to another farm. Go through a metal kissing gate and stay on the concrete path, ignoring the stile on the left, and join a tarmac driveway.

3 After about 140yd, turn left at a black metal fire and emergency gate, and head towards Triggs Lock.

4 Go over the lock gates and turn right along the towpath towards the bridge ahead.

5 There, turn left away from the canal, over a stile, aiming directly for Send Church. It is this area that may be flooded; if it is then you

will not be able to visit the church.

6 If conditions permit, go across the watermeadow and over the footbridge. Skirt a farmhouse to reach the church.

7 To return, retrace the route to Triggs Lock and continue ahead to go over the footbridge at the point where the river and canal join.

8 Now follow the river bank to reach Worsfold Gates where the river and canal diverge. There, follow the towpath back to the start.

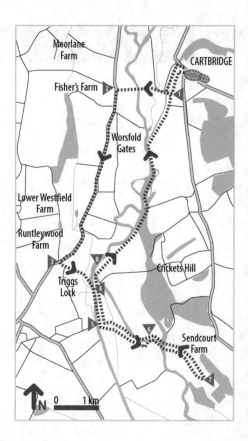

Points of interest

Send Church – The first record of a church in Send appears in The Domesday Book, compiled in 1085; the present building is a result of continuous changes since that date.

Worsfold Gates – The gates form a lock which is normally left open, but can be closed in times of flood. The gates are equipped with hand-drawn paddles, and the sluices are opened by pulling them up and inserting a peg to hold them open.

Thursley and Houndown

START At SU900398, car park near the cricket pitch, GU8 6QA

DISTANCE 3 miles (4.75km)

SUMMARY An easy walk on sandy tracks

PARKING Free parking at the start

MAPS OS Sheets Landranger 186; Explorer 133 and 145

WHERE TO EAT AND DRINK The Three Horseshoes, www.threehorseshoesthursley.com. Lovely country pub serving a high quality menu using locally sourced ingredients. Open daily 12:00–15:00; 17:30–23:00

A charming walk through woods and along an exposed trail with some pretty cottages towards the finish.

1 From the car park at the start, cross the grass by the children's play area to find a path below the cricket pitch. The path leads through trees and bracken to join a sandy bridleway running beside a field on the left. At a fork, bear left passing a corrugated barn to join a track leading to a road. Turn left.

2 Keep ahead at the next bend beside Truxford Cottage and signposted to 'October Farm'. Follow this lane to climb upwards and to find a car park at the crest.

3 Go through the car park and up the wooden steps. Bear left onto the wide sandy path. Over to the right is a substantial depression with military buildings at the bottom. Enjoy the views along this bridleway. Then descend on the ever-increasingly sandy path into a dip. Keep ahead up the rise and pass to the left side of a rounded hill.

4 At a path junction, take the second turning left.

5 Then take the left fork at the wooden post marked 'Ministry of Defence Red Route'. Keep straight ahead at a pylon within the conifers. Now drop down, joining other tracks that are all heading downwards for the bridge over a stream.

6 Bear left up the lane beyond to reach a road.

7 Go right for 100yd to the 'Slow' road marking.

8 Here, turn left down a path. Go over a bridge and descend through a gully to reach a picturesque stream.

9 Cross a stile and turn left along the drive ahead to reach a road. Turn right up the road between the cottages and at the bend take the path to go right up a gully.

10 Keep ahead below a bank of bracken and continue to reach a lane. Now, follow the lane past some charming cottages to reach the centre of the village.

11 Turn left to return to the start.

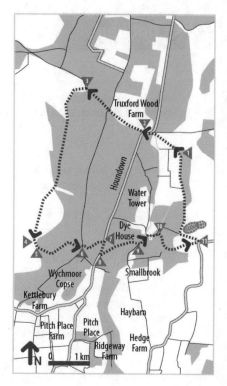

Points of interest

Thursley Common – One of few surviving areas of lowland peat bog in southern Britain providing a particularly rich habitat for dragonflies and damselflies along with many other species including the endangered woodlark and Dartford warbler. In July 2006 during a heat wave that affected southern England, 60% of the common was burnt. There have been several military camps in the parish. Between 1922 and 1957 Thursley Camp (from 1941 renamed Tweedsmuir Camp), to the north west of the village, housed British, Canadian and American forces at various times. On the 7th November 1942 it was bombed by the German air force. After World War II it was used to house displaced Poles. To the west was Houndown Camp that was used by the British Royal Marines.

Chobham

START At SU974619, the car park off Chobham High Street, GU24 8LY

DISTANCE 3¼ miles (5km)

SUMMARY Easy walking mainly along the riverbank and through paddocks

PARKING In the car park at the start

MAPS OS Sheets Landranger 176; Explorer 160

WHERE TO EAT AND DRINK Pasha Café and Delicatessen, www. pashachobham.co.uk. Great Turkish café serving delicious modern and traditional dishes. Open daily 08:00–17:00; Saturdays 09:00–17:00; Sundays 09:00–16:00

A pretty walk around the area of Chobham and close to Fairoaks Airport.

1 From the yellow barrier entrance to the car park, take the path that leads between a hedge and a fence, and bear left to the Mill Bourne stream. Walk along the riverbank path for 1¼ miles, crossing over a metal stile and driveway along the way, and finally emerging onto a road (Philpot Lane), beside Fairbourne Manor. From this point you can take a small detour to the left, going along the road as far as the hump-back bridge in order to enjoy the sight of the stream cascading around the small island at Emmetts Mill. Return to the point at which you emerged on to the road.

2 Walk past Fairbourne Manor to go through the gate on the far side of the grass frontage, beside the small clump of trees. Bear left and continue ahead through a series of paddocks, passing a ménage and stables on your left and negotiating two gates, one stile, a double stile and finally a metal kissing gate. Keep to the right of a line of conifers and, beyond a brick wall, enter another paddock and aim for the thatched house, Imlet Cottage, visible ahead, to reach a road.

3 Now turn right on the road. Walk down past Chobham Farm to reach a junction with the main road. Turn right and shortly turn right again along the public footpath signposted for 'Oaklands Cottage'.

4 Go past an old tennis court and cross a plank bridge and stile.

Cross the meadow beyond, and at the far side, go through the gate.

⑤ Turn left, heading for St Lawrence's Church.

⑥ Cross a stile and at a gate at the junction in front of the fenced cricket field, turn right to return directly to the car park.

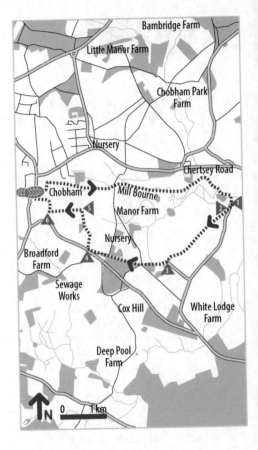

Points of interest

Fairoaks Airport – Fairoaks opened as a private airstrip in 1931, but was signed up for military use in 1936 and became RAF Fairoaks during World War II. It was used as a training airfield, with No. 18 Elementary & Reserve Flying School being formed on 1 October 1937 equipped with De Havilland Tiger Moths. 6,000 pilots were trained at the airfield.

Box Hill

START At TQ178513, National Trust Shop at top of Box Hill KT20 7LB

DISTANCE 3½ miles (5.5km)

SUMMARY A moderate walk due to tricky terrain at times

PARKING Free parking for National Trust members

MAPS OS Sheets Landranger 187; Explorer 146

WHERE TO EAT AND DRINK National Trust café and servery, www. nationaltrust.org.uk/box-hill/eating-and-shopping. Selling snacks, homemade sandwiches and cakes. Open daily

A walk around Surrey's most visited beauty spot and the part of the 2012 Olympic Cycle route.

1 Leaving the shop and information centre, turn right to the road and continue beside this to reach the view point. Take the path at the foot of the steps, walking in the direction of Hindhead. This is a section of the North Downs Way, marked with the acorn logo.

2 Once through a short wooded stretch and just beyond the end of the grass slope, the Way goes down to the left, but your route goes straight ahead following the orange and purple 'Hill Top Stroll' sign. The path curls clockwise, with Denbies Vineyard covering the hillside opposite and the spire of Ranmore church piercing the sky beyond. A stone placed in the middle of the path marks the grave of Major Peter Labellière. Beyond this, the walk commences a gradual descent on a chalky and uneven path and ignores the orange and purple sign on the right.

3 Just at the point where the chalk regains a grass covering and as the main path forks, look out for a small path on the right that leads you steeply down. In the distance you can see a bank with several trails and steps leading you to the Zig Zag Road. At the crossing track at the bottom of this steep path go straight over. Go down a long flight of steps to reach a point just above the Zig Zag Road.

4 Turn right to the hair-pin bend and walk up the grassy floor of the

valley. A short distance after crossing the road higher up, bear left to reach a wide track.

⑤ Then turn left. You are now on the 'Box Hill Hike' route. Keep ahead for just over ½ mile. Just after passing through a gate there is a fantastic view of Denbies Vineyard to the left.

⑥ After the next gate, and having reached Broadwood's Folly, turn right continuing to follow the 'Box Hill Hike' sign and continue through the woods.

⑦ After descending some steep steps, turn right to go up 'Juniper Bottom'.

⑧ At the top of the hill, you take the first path on the right marked with a blue topped post, but before doing so, take a moment to admire the impressive yew

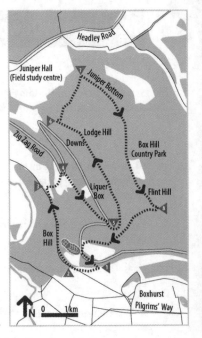

tree that is thought to be over 250 years old. Follow the path through the woods back to the start.

Points of interest

Viewing platform – The platform, situated at 564ft (172m), overlooks Dorking and Brockham. It commemorates the gift of Box Hill to the nation in 1914 by Leopold Salomons, who lived in Norbury Park.

Major Peter Labellière – The Major was an eccentric resident of Dorking. He requested that, on his death, he should be buried head downwards. This took place on 11 July 1800 when he died at the age of 75.

Broadwood's Folly – The tower was built by the piano maker Thomas Broadwood who purchased Juniper Hall in 1814. You can see the Juniper Hall Field Centre from the folly.

Mickleham Downs

START At TQ170534, The Running
Horses, Mickleham RH5 6DU

DISTANCE 3½ miles (5.5km)

SUMMARY Hard walking up to
Mickleham Downs using footpaths
and wooded trails

PARKING Ample parking on the road
near to the start point

MAPS OS Sheets Landranger 187;
Explorer 146

WHERE TO EAT AND DRINK The Running
Horses, www.therunninghorses.
co.uk. Food served Monday to Friday
12:00–14:30, 19:00–21:30; Saturday
12:00–15:00, 12:00–21:30 and
Sunday 12:00–18:00

The King William IV, www.
thekingwilliamiv.com. Good value,
traditional pub food served all day,
everyday. Open daily 11:00–23:00;
Sunday 12:00–22:30

A short circular walk taking in the grasslands of the Mickleham Downs and
with a couple of steep ascents.

1 From the Running Horses, go into St Michael's churchyard beside
The Rectory and walk alongside the Lloyd memorial wall. Turn left to
its end. Turn left and continue over the drive, following the red 'Box
Hill Hike' arrow, to reach a junction by a tall cottage gate.

2 Go right here, once again following the red arrow, and continue
along the lane beyond Lammas Cottage and several other houses to
reach Byttom Hill near the A24.

3 Turn right to pass The King William IV Inn and climb steadily for
around 200yd to reach a five-way junction (WP4).

4 Take the steep path beyond the metal gate and continue upwards
for just under ½ mile.

5 At the staggered junction, turn left following the blue bridleway
marker and then after a few yards turn right staying on the bridleway.
Continue through the woods until you come to a track after roughly 200yd.

6 Turn right and keep ahead until you reach the open space of the Mickleham Downs.

7 The walk goes right here, but before doing so it is worth exploring to your left to see the different terrain and landscape.

8 Back on the route and passing a blue marker post, head towards the woods. At a fork in the path, shortly after another blue marker post, bear left. You will see a triangulation marker tucked away in a corner by the path that was to the right. Continue on the left fork into the trees.

9 At the metal pole after approximately 60yd, turn left. Follow this track all the way down to reach a road with Juniper Hall opposite.

10 Turn right and return to the village initially using the footpath on the opposite side of the road hidden behind a hedge and then finishing on the pavement.

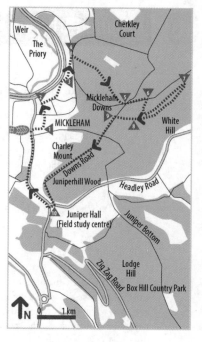

Points of interest

St. Michael's church – The original church, of which there are still traces inside this building, was a small Saxon one of nave and chancel only. On entering, look up behind you to see something of this Saxon work, which probably dates back to the year 950. One of the many interesting features is the 'Weeping Chancel'; common in ancient churches, it is an attempt to symbolize the inclined head of Christ upon the Cross.

Juniper Hall – Leased from the National Trust, Juniper Hall is a wonderful country house dating from the 18th century. Steeped in history, it opened as a field studies centre in 1947 and continues to provide an excellent facility for students to study the rich and varied surrounding environment.

Around Pirbright

START At SU946559, Pirbright Green pond, GU24 0JU

DISTANCE 3½ miles (5.5km)

SUMMARY An easy walk on mixed terrain

PARKING On-street parking available at the start

MAPS OS Sheets Landranger 186; Explorer 145

WHERE TO EAT AND DRINK The Cricketers Inn, Pirbright. www. cricketersinn.yolasite.com. The White Hart, Pirbright. www. thewhitehartpirbright.co.uk

An interesting and varied walk around the village of Pirbright.

1️⃣ Take the path running between The Cricketers Inn and Myrtle Cottage to pass through a wooden gate. At the end of the tarmac drive, keep ahead on the path for 20yd. Then turn right. Continue along the straight pathway through a plantation of fir trees and enter a wood. At the other end of the wood, cross a plank bridge and then head half-right across a field to reach Whites Farm.

2️⃣ Turn left along the drive past the tennis court, and then bear right to eventually meet a lane at Sandyburn.

3️⃣ Turn right and walk to Hogleys House. Now follow the path ahead to the immediate left of the building.

4️⃣ Cross the drive at the entrance to Hogleys Farm, and continue forward, passing behind the garden of Heath Farm House. A pleasant section of walking follows, going between heather-covered common and woodland to reach a junction.

5️⃣ Turn right and cross the wooden footbridge over a stream to reach a path that goes beside a garden.

6️⃣ At the drive to Bullswater Cottage, go forward for 50yd and then turn right beyond Heather Lodge to go along the drive to Springbok and

The Glade. The alley beyond leads to the main road; walk along the pavement for ¼ mile to reach the roundabout.

(7) On the opposite side of the road, by the oak tree and pond, take the driveway towards Cramond House. Just inside the trees, fork right onto a path running between fencing to emerge beside a paddock. Cross grassland and go through gates to reach a lane.

(8) Turn left, walking past Millcroft and The Glen and continue as far as the car parking area where the surfaced road ends.

(9) Bear right towards Brambles and then stay beside an old fence on a path that climbs above the drive to reach a field. Keep to the top side of the field, then descend beyond the gate to cross another field. The path beyond crosses a stream and joins a road.

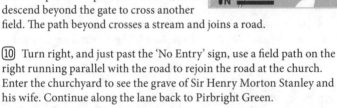

(10) Turn right, and just past the 'No Entry' sign, use a field path on the right running parallel with the road to rejoin the road at the church. Enter the churchyard to see the grave of Sir Henry Morton Stanley and his wife. Continue along the lane back to Pirbright Green.

Points of interest

Sir Henry Morton Stanley – Born to unmarried parents, Stanley was brought up in a workhouse. In 1859, at 18 years old, he left for New Orleans and took the name of a merchant, Henry Stanley. Stanley went on to serve on both sides in the American Civil War and then worked as a sailor and journalist. As special correspondent for the *New York Herald*, he was commissioned to go to Africa to search for Scottish missionary and explorer David Livingstone. Stanley reached Lake Tanganyika in November 1871 where he found the sick explorer, greeting him with the famous words, 'Dr Livingstone, I presume?' Stanley's reports on his expedition made his name.

Frensham and Batts Corner

START At SU842414, St Mary the Virgin church, GU10 3EA

DISTANCE 3½ miles (5.5km) or 5 miles (8km)

SUMMARY An easy walk on good trails and quiet lanes

PARKING Available on the street

Maps: OS Sheets Landranger 186; Explorer 145 and 133

WHERE TO EAT AND DRINK The Bluebell, Dockenfield. www.bluebell-dockenfield.com

Two pleasing walks taking in beautiful properties and on the longer route impressive views across Frensham Great Pond.

1 Go down the footpath outside the church wall to cross the River Wey using a wooden bridge. Continue up then go left along the lane at the top, passing The Malt House to reach a road.

2 Go straight across and up a drive, veering right opposite Sandpipers. Go through the gate then cross a stile. Bear left on a path along the edge of a field entering a small wood. On emerging from the wood, keep ahead, walking with trees to the right. After about 100yd, spot a stile in the hedgerow. Go over into woodland, ascending to reach a track running along the top side of a sloping field. Continue ahead to more woodland.

3 When the field on the left ends, fork half-right along a footpath. The path leads to a house. Near this, cross into the adjacent field.

4 Walk in front of the house to join a drive leading to a road. Turn left to reach the green and The Bluebell pub at Batts Corner.

5 Go down the lane passing the pub and follow it to reach Keepers Cottage. Fork right and keep ahead passing Bealeswood Cottage. Continue to reach a fork beyond the Old Cottage and Southfield.

6 Go left to join a bridleway leading to a road.

7 Turn left to reach a junction by a white house and bear right to

reach the River Wey. From this point the short walk continues along the road to return to the church.

For the longer walk, go through the gates of The Mill House, and take the track outside the wall beyond the wooden fence and gate. Follow the river until you reach a road, with Frensham Great Pond in front of you, and a hotel to the right.

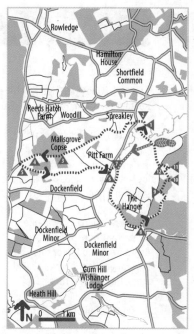

⑧ Turn left along the road (Bacon Lane) to reach a track which continues around the water's edge. Walk along the shore to reach a car parking area, head for the chalet which houses toilets, a snack bar and the ranger's office.

⑨ Go towards the car park entrance gate, but just before the entrance turn right along bridleway 45 by the white welcome sign. Keep on the bridleway for around 350yd until you reach a small crossroads with a blue bridleway sign and 'no cycling' signs on the left and right tracks.

⑩ Take the left track and follow the narrow gorse and heather fringed path upwards. Go up 2 steps and at the top of the climb, follow the path around to the right.

⑪ At the yellow arrowhead take the path left to go down to a road. Turn left for 35yd.

⑫ Then go right down a footpath to return to the church.

Points of interest

Frensham Great Pond and Frensham Little Pond were built in the Middle Ages to provide fish (especially carp) for the Bishop of Winchester's estate.

13 Headley Heath

START At TQ205548, Headley Hills Restaurant & Bar, Headley KT18 6LE

DISTANCE 3½ miles (5.5km)

SUMMARY A hard walk, often on loose stony ground, with some very steep inclines

PARKING Parking is available for patrons of the Headley Hills Restaurant and Bar or there are several public car parks available along this circular route

MAPS OS Sheets Landranger 187; Explorer 146

WHERE TO EAT AND DRINK The Cock Inn, Headley, www.cockinheadley.co.uk. Open from 11.00 for good food and drink at reasonable prices

An exploration of part of Headley Heath that continues steeply up to Mickleham Downs.

1 The Cock Inn, Headley, is located beside St Mary's church. Opposite the car park, take the public footpath by the bus stop. This brings you to a road by Ash House. Turn left up the road, and continue around the double bend. Great care should be taken as there is no pavement.

2 Opposite and just slightly to the left of The Mint House, go right to join a drive marked with a black private road 'The National Trust' sign. In the dip, by Garden Cottage, go up ahead, leaving the drive, which bears right. Continue straight ahead following this wide sand and stone track across Headley Heath. On reaching a blue bridleway marker post, keep ahead on the broad track.

3 This track soon rises to the top of a ridge where you take the first bridleway on your right, not the one closest to the inscribed plank bench. Go down on a wide, stony track following the blue bridleway marker post and passing a grassy slope on the right.

4 At the bottom, continue ahead, but just around the bend, turn right for a steep climb up a wooded bank.

5 At the top, go through a wooden gate and turn right in front of an ivy-clad wall. Make your way down to a road by Cockshott Cottage.

6 Cross the road and, avoiding the very steep ascent immediately ahead, take the path going left above the parking area. At the end of a level avenue of trees, bear right for the long uphill slog to reach Mickleham Downs. This is a grand strip of upland meadow, which extends for over ½ mile with a view to the spire of Ranmore Common church.

7 Turn right onto a track. Follow for just over ½ mile to reach a road almost opposite the entrance to Nower Wood Educational Nature Reserve.

8 Go right for 200yd.

9 Then turn left along another track. Beyond the cottage, continue to reach a road and go down to the bottom of the hill.

10 Just past The Tractor Shed on the right, go left through a kissing gate. Follow the track, going over two stiles.

11 Where the path splits bear right up a steep slope and another kissing gate to return to the start of the walk.

Points of interest

Nower Wood Educational Nature Reserve – Nower Wood is a Site of Nature Conservation Importance (SNCI). The predominant habitat at Nower Wood is ancient oak woodland which may date back as far as the Domesday Book. Although not open to the public, the reserve is managed to maximize the educational value for children and adults whilst keeping disturbance to the wildlife at a minimum. Many species of birds can be seen and occasionally adders are spotted. Roe deer, badgers and foxes have also been recorded.

Newlands Corner and Silent Pool

START At TQ044493, Newlands
Corner car park, GU4 8SE

DISTANCE 3½ miles (5.5km)

SUMMARY A hard walk due to steep
ascents and descents

PARKING Plenty available at the
start

MAPS OS Sheets Landranger 186
and 187; Explorer 145

WHERE TO EAT AND DRINK Tillings
Cornerhouse, www.tillingscafe.
co.uk. Scrummy toasties, pastries,
baguettes and drinks available daily
from 08:30–16:30

Challenging at times, this walk takes in part of the North Downs Way and the
mesmerizing Silent Pool.

1 From the car park, head to the A25 and follow the signs for the
North Downs Way. Cross the road and go through the barrier to
continue. After a mile, turn right following the 'Silent Pool' fingerpost.
Just after the path becomes chalky underfoot, there is an obvious
turn-off to the left, take a few steps to get the best view – beyond the
hillside the church in Shere can be spotted. Back on the downward
track, you will come across a WWII pill box on the left. This is one of
several that were built along the North Downs Way to protect London
from the Germans should they have invaded. Continuing on the
track, when the vineyard on the right comes into view, look out for
a turning on the left which leads you to some steps which descend to
Silent Pool. A path goes all the way around and, after exploring and
being fascinated by the unusual colour of the water, continue walking
to reach the A25.

2 Turn left for 100yd and cross the dual carriageway with care to the
A248. Head towards the church on the pavement behind the hedge.

3 At the crossing before the church itself, turn right across the road.
Go through a kissing gate and continue through fields and woods and
also the local landfill site. Here, join a track and continue until you
reach Timbercroft.

4 Keep ahead for roughly 600yd. At some cottages, continue down the track to a lane.

5 Take the steep path opposite, continue to reach a T-junction at the edge of woodland.

6 Bear right to head for the farmhouse, pass through the hedge and turn right. Climb up through the field.

7 At the top go through a gate. Keep climbing to reach the car park and the start of the walk.

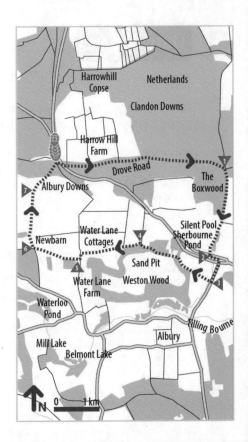

Points of interest

Silent Pool – A popular place to visit since Victorian times, Silent Pool is a lake of crystal clear water, with a beautiful blue green colour. A viewing platform enables easy access to the pond. Water feeding the lake comes from springs in the Downs' lower chalk. Natural filtration leaves the water completely clear. Numerous legends abound about Silent Pool, but perhaps the most famous story occurred in 1926 when, after Agatha Christie's car was found abandoned at the car park, a nationwide search began to find the author. Eleven days later she turned up in Harrogate, but never could explain the reason for her strange disappearance.

Outwood

Start At TQ327456, Outwood
Windmill, RH1 5PW

Distance 3½ miles (5.5km)

Summary An easy level walk mainly
across fields

Parking Available at the start

Maps OS Sheets Landranger 187;
Explorer 146

Where to eat and drink The Castle,
Wasp Green, www.castleoutwood.
co.uk

Straightforward walking with an opportunity to admire England's oldest
working windmill.

1️⃣ Walk along the green in the direction of Bletchingley and
Godstone for 50yd and turn left onto a track to pass by the cottages.
At the fork, keep ahead to reach Path End cottage. Follow the path
beyond through a belt of trees and over the crown of a hill. Maintain
the same direction through a succession of fields to reach a path
crossing in front of a farm.

2️⃣ Turn sharp left, heading for the gate beyond the bridge with
tubular railings. A gentle ascent now brings you to the end of the
fields. Continue along the brick and stone track to reach a junction
with overhead lines.

3️⃣ Turn right here and follow the path to reach a road. Take the
footpath across the road to skirt fields and to join the residential
Bellwether Lane. Go up the lane to a T-junction.

4️⃣ Turn left along the road, passing The Castle pub.

5️⃣ About 100yd beyond The Castle, go right up a grassy path to
reach a field from where there is a good view towards Gatwick
Airport. Now descend, going towards the overhead lines.

6️⃣ But turn left before them to go over three planks and a stile. Go up the side of a field and keep ahead to cross another plank bridge and a stile.

7 Maintain the same direction to reach a 3-way fingerpost and turn left.

8 50yd past the stile and metal gates, go right over the stile. Follow the path to reach the drive of Marl Pond Cottage, and continue to reach the road.

9 Turn left to return to the windmill.

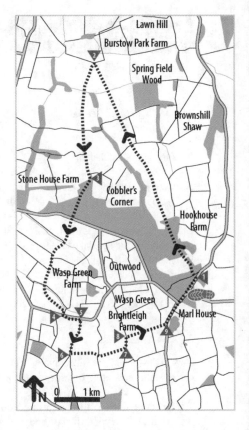

Points of interest

Outwood Windmill – The oldest working windmill in the country. The village of Outwood acquired its name at a time when many people were leaving London and heading for cleaner country air. Some of those came to live 'Out in the Wood', which eventually became 'Outwood'. The windmill began turning wheat into flour during the early years of the reign of Charles II and is still doing so to this day.

Peaslake to Pitch Hill

Start At TQ086447, Peaslake Village Stores GU5 9RL

Distance 3½ miles (5.5km)

Summary Easy walking on mainly sandy woodland trails

Parking Some parking is available on the road at the Peaslake Village Stores or plenty is available for free at the Hurtwood Control Car Park 2 which is near the start and forms part of the walk

Maps OS Sheets Landranger 187; Explorer 145

Where to eat and drink Peaslake Village Stores, www. peaslakevillagestores.com. Good deli counter, the cheese straws are legendary. Open daily till 18:30, Sun till 17:00

The Hurtwood Inn, www. hurtwoodinn.com. Italian bar/ restaurant serving snacks and pizzas at moderate prices. Drinks all day, food available 09:00–11:30, 12:00–14:30, 18:00–21:30

Walk to the top of Pitch Hill for magnificent views, using shady, sometimes narrow paths and return on wide sandy tracks.

1 Start out along Walking Bottom, going past the Hurtwood Inn on your right. Just beyond the last house on the road, bear left and pass through Hurtwood Control Car Park 2 and the two concrete blocks near the Hurtwood Control notice board. Stay on the main track, gaining height easily, for just under a mile. There are several crossing tracks on the way, ignore these.

2 Look out for a fork where the paths divides at a cluster of three trees. Bear left here and follow the track upwards. After a further ½ mile, you are rewarded with views to the south as you emerge from the woodland.

3 Turn right and after roughly 100yd take the left path marked with a 'Footpath Only' barrier. Continue until a T-junction where you turn right and continue until you see the triangulation pillar marking the highest point of Pitch Hill, at 843ft (257m). Rest here and enjoy the

far-reaching views on the green metal bench dedicated to Murray Carson OBE.

4 Retrace your steps until you come to a slight incline, which will lead you to another metal bench. Stay on the main path until you reach a wide sandy bridleway.

5 Turn left onto this bridleway and keep ahead from now on. Ignoring all paths to the left and right, after 1¼ miles you will reach the cemetery.

6 Follow the pathway in front of the lych gate down to St Mark's church from where it is only a short walk back to the start.

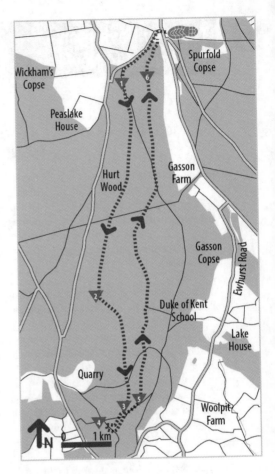

Points of interest

Pitch Hill – The hill is the most westerly of the three summits in this range. Leith Hill is the highest at 965ft (294m), while in between, both in terms of height and location is Holmbury Hill, 857ft (261m).

17 The Wey Navington – Weybridge to New Haw

START At TQ068647, Town Lock KT13 8XX

DISTANCE 3½ miles (5.5km)

SUMMARY An easy walk along a lower stretch of the canal

PARKING Free street parking can be found nearby

MAPS OS Sheets Landranger 187; Explorer 160

WHERE TO EAT AND DRINK The Queen's Head, www.whitebrasserie.com/ locations/weybridge.html. Pleasant pub with a smart brasserie. Open daily 11:00–23:00; Sundays 12:00–22:00

A circular walk taking in part of the Wey Navigation and the River Wey in close proximity to the smart town of Weybridge.

The two walks from Weybridge both commence at Town Lock, which is a short distance down Bridge Road from its junction at the end of Church Street (see Walk 88 for the other).

1 Set off along the towpath with the Navigation on your left. After ¼ mile you come to Blackboys Footbridge; go over it and continue along the towpath. Pass under the low railway bridge to reach Coxes Lock and Coxes Mill.

2 A further ¾ mile brings you to the road at New Haw.

3 Follow the road to the left, around the bend.

4 Take the footpath on the left.

5 Turn left at the T-junction and keep ahead to reach Wey Manor Farm. Here, you may want to walk forward to the railway embankment to have a look at Nine Arches bridge over to the left, and also to see the ponds just down the other side; if you do, return to the farm to continue the walk. Follow the well-made wide track in front of the

cottage and around a series of turns for just over ½ mile.

6 At a fork immediately beneath power lines, bear right to reach the railway embankment. Go left on the other side, skirting the Riverside Park homes. Follow the drive between the brick pillars, and later beside the River Wey, to return to the start where the river and Navigation unite.

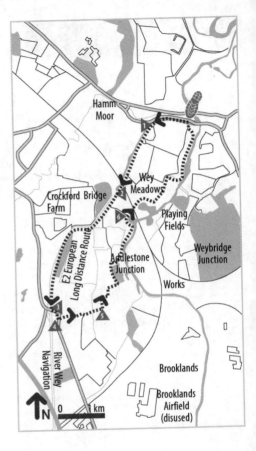

Points of interest

Coxes Lock Mill – Three closely-grouped mill buildings which were a mixture of industrial mill and foundry and accommodation for 207 years. Shortly after the closure of the mills in 1983 and the ceasing of commercial traffic, the navigation was donated to the National Trust. The three mill buildings are now apartments but are listed Grade II for heritage or architecture.

Abinger Roughs

Start At TQ110479, Abinger Roughs National Trust car park, RH5 6BF

Distance 3¾ miles (6km)

Summary A hard walk due to a steep ascent and descent

Parking Free parking at the start

Maps OS Sheets Landranger 186; Explorer 146

Where to eat and drink Provisions can be bought in nearby Abinger Hammer; there are no refreshments stops en route

An energetic walk through mixed woodland and on chalk and flint trails, the magnificent views are worth the effort.

① At the far end of the car park, go through the wooden barrier and straight ahead on the descending path. At the T-junction, turn left to continue on the wide trail up the hill.

② At an open grassy area, take the right path signposted with a blue arrow and Public Bridleway and descend down through the woods.

③ As you exit the woods, turn right onto a track and follow it over a railway bridge. Continue past a farm on the right, through a gate onto a grassy, chalk and flint track.

④ At the top of the track, fork left following the bridleway and continuing uphill.

⑤ At the T-junction at the crest of the ascent turn right to continue uphill.

⑥ As you exit the woodland and come to a grassy patch, bear right to join the North Downs way, signposted with an acorn and a yellow arrow. Pass through a gate and continue along the ridge. Take a moment to admire the magnificent view to the south from Blatchford Down.

⑦ Continue through a gate into woodland, staying on the undulating

North Downs Way eventually dropping down to a road.

⑧ Cross the road and follow the chalk and flint path around to the left. As you exit the woods, and with great care, take an immediate path down to the right with a cream house ahead in the distance.

⑨ At the bottom of the grassy slope, follow the path around to the right. Carry on until you reach a gate.

⑩ Pass through the gate and keep ahead to go over the railway line.

⑪ At the junction of paths by the cream house, turn right to follow the Public Bridleway between two barns. You are now on National Cycle Route 22. Continue for just over ½ mile until you reach a road. Cross and continue on National Cycle Route 22, re-entering the Abinger Roughs.

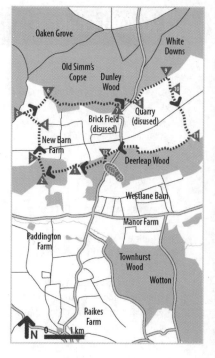

⑫ At the Samuel Wilberforce monument, turn left for a short climb back to the car park.

Points of interest

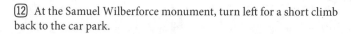

Samuel Wilberforce monument – The son of the politician and anti-slavery philanthropist William Wilberforce, he was ordained an Anglican priest in 1829 and in 1845 was appointed Bishop of Oxford. A frequent critic of liberal bishops, dissenters, and biblical scholars, Wilberforce attacked Charles Darwin's theory of evolution in an exchange with the biologist Thomas Huxley in 1860 and was generally viewed as the loser of the debate. He died aged 67 after a shock fall from his horse at the site of the monument.

Around Chaldon

START At TQ308557, Chaldon church, CR3 5AF

DISTANCE 3¾ miles (6km)

SUMMARY An easy level walk mostly through farmland

PARKING Available at the church

MAPS OS Sheets Landranger 187; Explorer 146

WHERE TO EAT AND DRINK Nothing en route, but Fanny's Farm Shop in Merstham is worth a visit. www.fannysfarm.com

A gentle walk in the area around Chaldon with a lofty view of some impressive South-East infrastructure!

1 From the churchyard entrance, walk up to reach a stile just before the approach to Court Farm. Go over the stile and cross three fields to enter a wood. Go left along an old concrete pathway to reach a road and a 'Farm Traffic' warning triangle, enter the field on the opposite side of the road.

2 Go diagonally across the field to rejoin the road at Alderstead Farm.

3 Turn left along the road, passing the water compound and bearing right downhill.

4 Opposite Windfield (WP4), turn left down steps and follow the path out into the open country. From here there is an interesting view down to the M23 and its junction with M25, Surrey's very own 'Spaghetti Junction'. Follow the path across several fields to reach a chalky track just up from a house at Tollsworth Manor Farm.

5 Turn right here to join the North Downs Way. Follow the Way, also signposted 'Downlands Circular Walk' to reach a road opposite Hilltop Farm. Turn left along Hilltop Lane for 75yd.

6 Then go right beside a house named Pilgrims Lodge. Now cross

a succession of stiles and fields to reach Five Ways Crossing, which is marked with a prominent finger post.

⑦ Follow the path signed for 'Rook Lane'.

⑧ Cross the Lane (the B2031) to reach Doctors Lane and follow it downhill.

⑨ At the bottom, take the right turn to soon bring you back to Chaldon church.

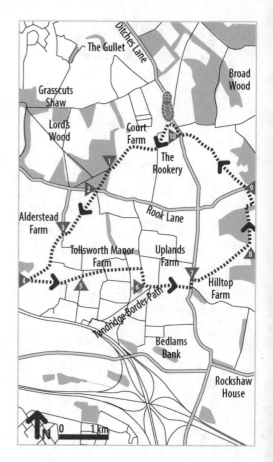

Points of interest

Chaldon church – The church contains the earliest known English wall painting, dating from the 12th century. It is believed to have been the work of a travelling monk and depicts 'The Ladder of Salvation of the Human Soul'. The square bowl of the font was carved by hand out of a single block of locally quarried Merstham stone.

Start At TQ176437, Beare Green pond, near Holmwood station, Beare Green RH5 4RB

Distance 3¾ miles (6km)

Summary Easy level walking between farms, a fishery and a prestigious stables

Parking Plenty of roadside parking available

Maps OS Sheets Landranger 187; Explorer 146

Where to eat and drink The Duke's Head, www.dukesheadbearegreen. co.uk. Food served daily 12:00–15:00 and 18:00–22:00; Sundays 12:00–17:00.

A gentle walk between two villages using wooded trails, farmland, drives and roads.

1 Walk up the road towards the station and turn right at the public bridleway signposted 'leading to Bregsells Farm'. Pass under the A24 and continue through the farmyard into fields via the metal gate. Keeping the railway line to your left, continue and halfway through the third field a corrugated roof comes into view. Head towards it and continue past the derelict building to reach a road.

2 Turn right past the entrance to Petersfield Farm.

3 Shortly after turn left along the concrete drive to Oakwood House. Walk past the farm building of Swires Farm. Stay on the track, following it round an s-bend, until you reach a grassy area.

4 At this junction, take the track round to the right, following the 'Public Bridleway' signpost. Keep the hedgerow on your immediate right all the way to the edge of the next field.

5 At the corner, turn right along a grass strip, still staying beside the hedgerow.

6 At the end of the field, the grass continues ahead into woodland

and bracken. As you enter, take the public footpath on the right. Keep to the narrow path through the bracken and cross the assault course track. Continue straight ahead until you emerge at a tree with a yellow 'Landowners Welcome Caring Walkers' footpath sign.

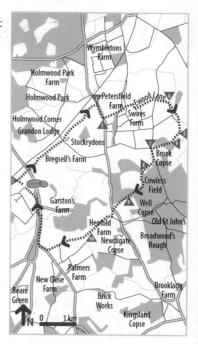

7 Turn left here and follow the path to a right turn over a wooden plank bridge. Keep to the left, cross a stile and continue to pass a pond on your left.

8 Once across the ford, keep ahead to skirt another pond. The path enters woodland. Go straight ahead into the woodland and keep on the broad track passing some huts on your right. Stay on this uphill path until you reach a wooden post.

9 Take the left fork. Keep going until you reach a road. Cross the road to Henfold House and turn right in front of the white gate. Beyond the wooden barn, turn left to walk beside the garden pond. You will soon come to the horse riding circuit; cross this opposite a small seat on the left and the gate leading from the lawn. Now go down the grass between the fences and cross the horse-ride again at the bottom. Walk ahead, going through three fields to reach a road.

10 Turn right to reach the Duke's Head Inn on the A24, and then continue with care beside the busy road to reach a subway returning you to Beare Green pond.

Points of interest

Henfold House Stables is a National Hunt racing yard with an impressive history. The yard prepares horses for races with a range of private grass and all-weather gallops, schooling grounds, turn-out paddocks and quiet wooded tracks.

START At TQ397415, Dormans railway station, RH7 6NL

DISTANCE 3¾ miles (6km)

SUMMARY An easy walk on quiet roads, leafy trails, a golf course and a racecourse

PARKING Available on the road by the station

MAPS OS Sheets Landranger 187; Explorer 146

WHERE TO EAT AND DRINK Nothing en route, but nearby Dormansland has a village shop and pubs

A mainly level walk taking in some grand houses and a most impressive viaduct.

① From the railway station, take the surfaced path running beside the station house. When a crossing at the entrance to Nobles is reached, turn left. Cross the railway bridge and turn left immediately, crossing a golf course and reaching Lingfield Park Racecourse.

② Go straight over the racecourse, down some steps and use the plank bridge to continue across the golf course to reach a road. Turn right and follow the road to a junction.

③ There, take the road signed for 'Felcourt' (Blackberry Road).

④ After about 200yd, turn left and follow the driveway to pass a barn. Continue ahead, going up the grassland to reach the entrance to some woodland close to a large garden.

⑤ Turn left down the line of pines. Cross a stream and take a rising shady path to reach a road.

⑥ Turn right to enter Dormans Park. Follow the road through the Park, ignoring all turnings to the left, to reach The Clock House.

⑦ Beyond the house the road narrows to a path; stay with the path, following it to where it ends, just before Felcourt Road.

[8] Turn left and walk past the second house (Wadlands). Then turn right along a cindered path.

[9] Stay on this path to a point about 75yd short of an arched railway bridge.

[10] There, turn left and walk along the edge of Wilderness Lake. The view in this section of the walk includes not only the lake, but the impressive Cooks Pond Viaduct. Continue along the path after it has left the lake, following the railway all the way back to Dormans station.

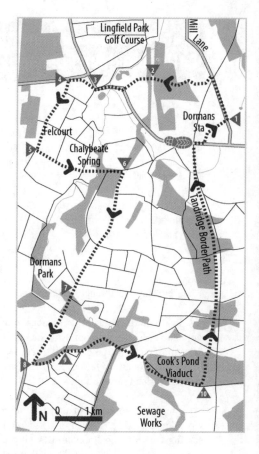

Points of interest

Cooks Pond Viaduct – A mainline railway bridge on the Oxted line crossing Wilderness Lake (originally called Cooks Pond). It is a wrought-iron girder construction on brick piers and has five spans of 125ft (37m) each. It is the largest structure on the Croydon to East Grinstead railway. The lake was drained temporarily whilst the piers were built.

Effingham Junction and Little Bookham Common

START At TQ102558, Effingham Junction railway station, KT24 5HX

DISTANCE 3¾ miles (6km)

SUMMARY Easy walking in a mixture of woodland trails, open fields, quiet roads and firm tracks

PARKING Plenty of parking in the station car park. Free on Sunday

MAPS OS Sheets Landranger 187; Explorer 146

WHERE TO EAT AND DRINK There are no refreshments stops en route, but provisions can be bought in nearby Cobham, Bookham or East Horsley

A level circular walk through woodland, common land and fields.

1️⃣ Begin on the road at the entrance to the station car park. Turn right and cross the road opposite the bus shelter. Turn left along a drive marked 'Private Road' and 'Permissive Footpath/Permissive Bridleway', but after a few yards, turn right onto a public footpath marked with a yellow arrow.

2️⃣ Emerging from a wood after ¼ mile, cross the stile by the second metal gate on the left, marked 'public footpath'. Continue passing a lawn-fringed pond until you reach a stile leading you to a strip of grassland divided by a channel, with a variety of interesting wild plants including bulrushes on your right. Go through the low railway arch; you may find llamas grazing in the fields beyond!

3️⃣ Soon you will arrive at a track at the end of more woodland. Turn right to pass the National Trust sign for 'Bank's Common' and continue. Banks Cottage is the brick house through the trees on the left. Carry on past Ivy Cottage. At the National Trust sign for 'Bookham Common', keep right on the track.

4️⃣ Cross the cattle grid. After having passed the thatched house Oak

Tree Cottage, The White House and Little Bookham Allotments, you will eventually come to a junction.

⑤ Proceed right along Maddox Lane and cross the railway bridge.

⑥ Immediately beyond, turn right along a footpath backing onto houses on the left. At the field at the bottom, cross the stile and head towards the wooden bridge with unusual built-in stiles, diagonally opposite.

⑦ Use this bridge and continue to join a track in the next field. Go through two metal gates and head for the house named Honeypots.

⑧ Walk along the avenue and cross the main road at its end.

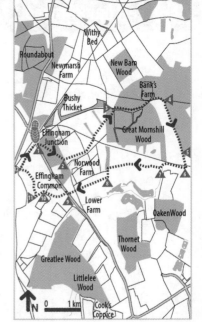

⑨ Continue by going along the drive to Squirrels and Tyrells, then bearing right through a copse to reach the cricket pitch. Pass in front of the pavilion and scoreboard.

⑩ At the nets cross the stile under the trees. Go straight ahead to reach a path at the edge of the wood.

⑪ Turn right and head towards the bungalows in the distance and a wooden sign marked 'Effingham Common'.

⑫ Turn right through the trees to reach the station car park.

Points of interest

Effingham Junction – Provides a popular commuter route to London Waterloo and to Guildford in the opposite direction.

Fetcham Downs

START At TQ152549, Norbury car park at the top of the Leatherhead by-pass, KT22 9DX

DISTANCE 3¾ miles (6km)

SUMMARY An easy walk alongside fields and through woodland

PARKING Car park at the start of the walk

MAPS OS Sheets Landranger 187; Explorer 146

WHERE TO EAT AND DRINK Old Barn Tearooms, Bocketts Farm, www. bockettsfarm.co.uk. Open daily from 1:000–17:30 serving well-priced traditional cakes, lunches and cream teas

Gently undulating with some wonderful views of London to the north and Box Hill to the south.

1 Turn off the drive to Bocketts Farm immediately past the top car park, walking along the track that is heading for the sawmill. Just after going around a bend, take the right branch at a fork onto a Public Byway going under a canopy of trees. When a path crossing is reached, go ahead.

2 At the end of the field, bear left into a copse and through the staggered fence onto a public footpath. Emerge onto the bridleway and continue left, passing a bench at the field's edge with magnificent views to London.

3 At the fork almost at the bottom, take the right public bridleway going up the side of a field, with Bookham Wood on your right. At the top, walk into woodland and continue ahead on the track; it will become narrower as you walk along the edge of a field on your left. The path levels out as you continue past a metal gate and a mobile phone mast station; as it starts to descend, the spire of Ranmore church comes into view.

4 Just as you enter more woodland, and at the crossroads of the bridleway and footpath, turn left and follow the path to reach Crabtree

Cottages, from where there is a fine view to Box Hill and beyond.

⑤ Now turn left along the track signposted to Bookham, and follow it for around ¾ mile to reach a fork in the valley and a single bar gate.

⑥ Bear right and continue to Roaringhouse Farm. Ignore the major left turn here and keep ahead to reach the next path junction.

⑦ Now turn up left onto the signposted bridleway and follow the path back to the car park.

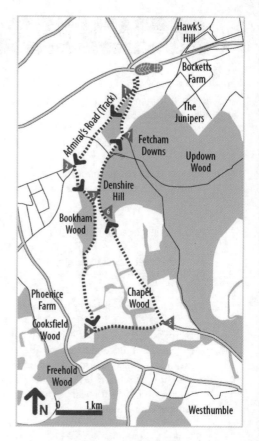

Points of interest

Views – North and beyond Leatherhead, the complete profile of London can be seen in the distance, from the arch of Wembley Stadium in the west right through to the skyscrapers of Canary Wharf to the east. The view south from Crabtree Cottages extends from Box Hill on the left across the Mole Gap, in which Dorking lies, to the continuation of the North Downs, where the spire of the church on Ranmore Common is prominent.

Godstone and Tandridge

START At TQ350515, Godstone Green Pond, RH9 8DY

DISTANCE 3¾ miles (6km)

SUMMARY Easy walking through farmers' fields and along country lanes

PARKING Village car park at the start

MAPS OS Sheets Landranger 187; Explorer 146

WHERE TO EAT AND DRINK White Hart, Godstone, www.beefeater.co.uk/steak-restaurant/Surrey/White-Hart-Godstone.html

The Bell, Godstone, www.thebellgodstone.co.uk

The Barley Mow, Tandridge, www.barleymowtandridge.co.uk

A gentle and level walk taking in four ponds.

1 From the pond, cross the road and proceed along the right side of the White Hart. Beyond the barn/village hall, you pass Bay Pond and come to St Nicholas' church. Go under the lych gate and to the right of the church itself. Leave the cemetery and descend to reach another pond. Beyond, the path bears right to approach an avenue of conifers leading to a pink house.

2 Bear left uphill to reach an open field. There, turn right and walk down to a drive, continuing alongside a long brick building.

3 Go past an old-fashioned lamp post and shortly afterwards turn right heading down to a lake.

4 At the bridleway signpost, turn left to cross a wooden bridge and skirt Leigh Mill House.

5 At the garages, take the gravelled bridleway to the right to pass the tennis court, and turn left between the hedges at the bottom. Follow the paling fence above another pond and keep straight ahead to reach a gate leading to the busy main road (A22).

6. Cross the road with care and head across several fields to reach a road near Tandridge. Just to the right here is the Barley Mow, but the route goes left and uphill through the village.

7. At a road junction, turn left into Jackass Lane and go down the lane as far as Little Court Farm with its belltower.

8. Here, take the bridleway to the left and follow this down to reach Hop Garden Cottage.

9. Take the underpass under the A22 and keep ahead to pass the brick building seen on the outward route. At the end of the brick wall and at the start of the fencing, carry on left along the track and pass the entrance gates to Leigh Place.

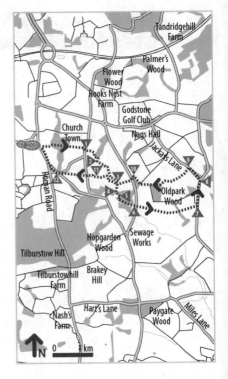

10. At the T-junction by Old Packhouse Cottage, go up the steps ahead to reach a field. Bear left to the crown of the field and then drop down to reach a lane. Go left along the lane to reach a road.

11. Turn right and follow the road back to Godstone Green.

Points of interest

St Nicholas' church – The prominent lych gate was erected in memory of G.E.G. Hoare; members of this family served the parish between 1821 and 1930. Restored in 1978, almost all of the windows date from the 19th century apart from one new window depicting the village past and present, given by the villagers of Godstone to mark the new millennium.

Oxshott Heath and Esher Common

START At TQ142611, car park near the station, KT22 0ZS

DISTANCE 3¾ miles (6km)

SUMMARY An easy walk mainly through woodland

PARKING Free parking at the start

MAPS OS Sheets Landranger 187; Explorer 161

WHERE TO EAT AND DRINK There are no refreshments stops en route

A generally level walk through, taking in the easy terrain of Oxshott Heath and Esher Common.

1 From the car park, take the Public Bridleway signposted to 'Browns Corner'. Pass some cottages and follow the blue arrowheads straight ahead until you reach the road at Browns Corner. Turn right at Browns Corner, taking the path on the left running parallel with the horse-ride and in the direction of Sandy Lane.

2 At a clearing with a notice board, turn left. Go through a barrier between the wooden fences to reach a road (The Ridings).

3 Turn right.

4 At the road end, follow the path going half-left beside Silver Greys and Fairview. At the end of the path, turn left onto a wide trail that leads you to West Bridge. Cross the A3.

5 Once over the bridge turn left signposted towards the 'Portsmouth Road'.

6 At a fork follow the yellow arrow signposted towards 'Black Pond'.

7 At the junction after the pond, turn right onto a path that leads into an avenue of pine trees. At the next junction turn right to head for the 'Five Ways' signpost in the clearing.

8 Follow the trail to 'Esher Common' and 'Arbrook Common'.

The cindered track passes through the middle of a cleared area and eventually turns to sand.

⑨ At the crossroads, turn right to re-cross the A3, this time via East Bridge. Drop down past a small pond on your left. Keep ahead to reach a road beside Roundhill Way on your right. Cross the road with care and climb up the path immediately behind the wooden stumps.

⑩ Continue through the woods following the 'Trail 2000' white arrows until you come to a T-junction where there is a splendid view ahead.

⑪ Turn left here and continue to reach the War Memorial.

⑫ Turn right to go down the broad steps.

⑬ Go left at the bottom to return to the car park.

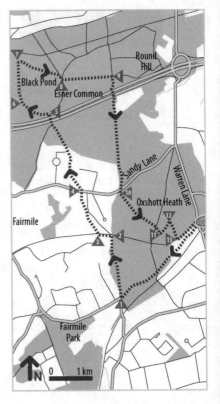

Points of interest

Oxshott Heath War Memorial – The Heath has many well-known landmarks. The sandpit was originally formed by the commercial demand for building sand in the latter part of the 19th century, but was used again in WWII as a source of sand for sandbags. The war memorial was, after some controversy, erected at the top of the south slope by Sir Robert McAlpine, then a resident of Fairmile Court. It affords one of the best views in Surrey on a clear day. Much clearance work was done around the War Memorial in time for the WWI Centenary Service in 2014, so that it is once again visible from different parts of the Heath.

START AAt TQ325605, Riddlesdown car park, CR8 1EE

DISTANCE 3¾ miles (6km)

SUMMARY A moderate walk due to a fairly steep, but easy underfoot, halfway climb

PARKING In the car park at the start

MAPS OS Sheets Landranger 187; Explorer 146 and 161

WHERE TO EAT AND DRINK Nothing en route

Keep an eye out for grazing sheep and cattle whilst walking in this chalk, scrub and grassland area of the London Borough of Croydon.

1 Leave the car park along the path and keep ahead, passing houses on your left. By the last house, turn left through a gate and go up to the road, then turn right. At a bend, go left towards the school.

2 Turn right along a bridleway before the electricity sub-station. Keep ahead at the end of the playing field and follow a level and fairly straight path to meet a road.

3 Turn right, passing the main entrances to the schools.

4 At the beginning of the grass verge, turn right through a gate. Go down into a wood beyond the grass, and, after a few yards, take the right-hand path, which descends quite steeply, to reach a large recreation area with tennis courts.

5 Find the fork in the obvious surfaced path near to the children's enclosed play areas.

6 Walk away from the play areas and the pavilion, keeping a red bin to your left.

7 Just before a railway arch, turn right to continue on the path through the trees, walking parallel with the railway line. A stiff ascent eventually brings you to fencing surrounding a deep, disused chalk pit.

Go anti-clockwise around this to reach a gate.

⑧ Turn left and aim for the picnic table and seat.

⑨ Now fork half-left in the direction of the metal tower on the opposite ridge above the houses.

⑩ Go between two five-bar gates and wire fencing. Go down the slope to reach a gate.

⑪ Turn right and follow a level path across an area of rough grassland to reach a fenced grazing area.

⑫ You will now merge with a main track coming up from the left. Walk gently uphill back to the start.

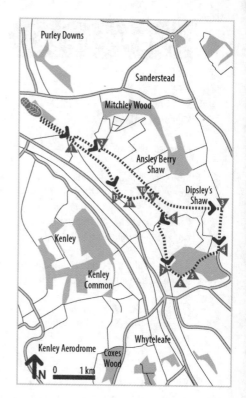

Points of interest

Riddlesdown – Most of Riddlesdown Common is a biological Site of Special Scientific Interest (SSSI). It is the largest area of calcareous scrub in Greater London, with a herb-rich chalk grassland, and is one of the few places in London with *Juniperus communis*.

Waggoners Wells

START At SU873353, Grayshott War
Memorial, GU26 6LF

DISTANCE 3¾ miles (6km)

SUMMARY A moderate walk due to a
steep incline towards the end

PARKING Available for free in the
village car park near to the start

MAPS OS Sheets Landranger 186;
Explorer 133

WHERE TO EAT AND DRINK The Fox &
Pelican, Grayshott,
www.foxandpelican.co.uk

A cross-border stroll into Hampshire passing through delightful woodlands
to see picturesque ponds and a charming wishing well.

① From the War Memorial, walk down Hill Road, passing the social
club, then turn right, following the blue arrowheads, into Stoney
Bottom.

② At the foot of the slope, beyond the last bungalow The Old
Yew Tree Cottage, go right along a track. After ¼ mile, fork left at a
pumping station, turning right after a further 75yd.

③ Follow the woodland path to reach a road which leads into a car
park. Turn right at the road and cross the ford.

④ Then bear left following the yellow arrowhead to walk beside the
ponds known as Waggoners Wells. Follow the path beyond the third
pond for 100yd to reach a brick house, Summerden.

⑤ Bear left here to find the Wishing Well and Lord Tennyson's 1863
poem 'Flower in the Crannied Wall' which was written at this site.

⑥ By means of the bridge return to the first pond and path on the
other side. Go up a staircase into the car park. Leave the car park by
the vehicle exit and turn right onto the wide track. Keep on this wide
track for 10yd.

7 Fork left ignoring the signposted 'Bridleway and Byway' on the right. Ascend gently on the wide moss-bordered track to reach a crossing opposite Mount Alvernia Wood.

8 Turn left up the steep slope to reach the end of a residential road. Keep ahead on a now level path.

9 Just as you start to descend, turn right, then fork left to drop down to the track which formed part of your outward route. Turn right, joining the surfaced part of Stoney Bottom and continue to reach the junction at the topcs.

10 Turn left to return to the War Memorial with the spire of St Luke's church straight ahead.

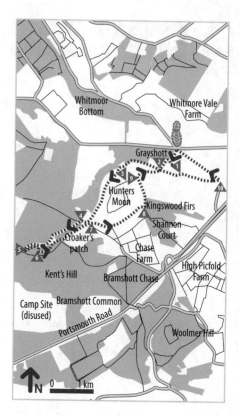

Points of interest

Waggoners Wells – These are a series of large ponds linked by streams and waterfalls created in the 17th Century and believed to be intended as hammer ponds to serve the local iron industry. It was acquired by the National Trust in 1919 and dedicated to the memory of Sir Robert Hunter (1844–1913) the founder of The National Trust in 1895.

Bowlhead Green

Start At SU917383, the crossroads in Bowlhead Green, GU8 6NW

Parking On the grass verge by the crossroads

Distance 4 miles (6.5km)

Maps OS Sheets Landranger 186; Explorer 133

Summary A moderate walk through fields, woodland and along pretty lanes

Where to eat and drink None en route

Take your time to admire some delightful cottages and impressive country houses on this quaint walk.

1 From the crossroads walk along the 'No Through Road'. At the fork, bear right to reach the gates of Lower House. Turn left, joining the Greensand Way. Continue ahead to cross a drive and go up the brick steps opposite. Turn right around the field. Go over a stile, and bear left to reach a road. Cross and continue, dropping down quite steeply. After descending the stone steps, walk beside a wall. Go past a pretty pond on your left and Cosford Farm on your right.

2 At the bend in the drive, turn left and keep ahead to walk past a barn and Hole Cottage and continue.

3 At the crossing by the farm entrance go left. Keep ahead at the fork, then drop down to reach a pond. Continue along the track for around ¼ mile to reach a U-bend.

4 There, go right towards Blackhanger Farm. Soon after crossing a stream, go left over a stile and skirt the house and garden of the farm. Follow the overhead lines across the next field, exiting in the left-hand corner.

5 Enter the woodland ahead beside a rusty iron P gate. Cross the stile in front and follow the footpath to cross the stream on a three-plank bridge. Continue until a road is reached.

6 Turn left along the road.

7 After 80yd, go left at the fork towards Emley. Continue past another charming house, Halnacker Cottage.

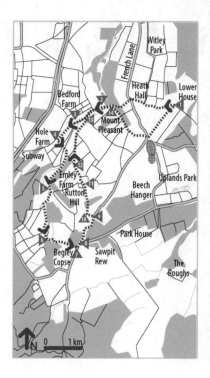

8 Beyond the cottage you turn left along the drive to Halnacker Hill.

9 Before the crest of the hill, turn off right. Climb up through the trees to the top of Rutton Hill. Continue down the other side of the hill, heading towards the red tiles of Emley Farm.

10 Turn left in front of the house and then go right through a tunnel of holly to reach a stile. Cross and veer left downhill.

11 At a fork by another P gate, go right, crossing the centre of the field. Follow the footpath to emerge on to the hillside above Hole Cottage. Go downhill from here.

12 At the far left corner, turn right. Now retrace the outward route passing Cosford Farm and the pond.

13 However, at the post, leave the outward route, bearing right onto a bridleway and staying outside the wood. This path climbs steadily to eventually return to the start.

Points of interest

P Gates – The iron gate bearing a star, coronet and letter P, were erected by Lord Pirrie of Witley Park after he had been created a Viscount.

Churt and Whitmoor Vale

START At SU855382, Churt crossroads, GU10 2JS

DISTANCE 4 miles (6.5km)

SUMMARY A moderate walk along woodland trails and lanes but with some steep descents and ascents

PARKING On the road at the start

MAPS OS Sheets Landranger 186; Explorer 133

WHERE TO EAT AND DRINK The Crossways Inn, Churt, www.weydonian.net/crossways

A charming woodland walk, crossing into Hampshire.

① Take the Headley/Bordon road opposite the Crossways Inn and walk down to the Thames Water pumping station. Go left and walk uphill. At a fork, bear right along a bridleway to pass Barford Mill.

② When the track curls right towards a house, keep ahead on a path above the lake. Continue past a cluster of houses nestling in a clearing to reach a road at the end of the drive. Now go forward for 200yd.

③ Immediately before a house named Woodland View, turn right and descend steeply to cross the stream. Climb up to a road and turn left.

④ Just after passing a house called Dingley Dell, take the path branching half-right up the slope and follow it to the top. Turn right.

⑤ At the fork just beyond the overhead lines and metal gate, bear right. Keep ahead for a straight and gradual descent.

⑥ At the T-junction, take the bridleway to the left to approach a road.

⑦ However, before reaching it, turn sharp right in front of a gate and then bear left after 20yd. Cross a stile to reach the entrance to Walnut Well.

⑧ Before the road, cross its drive and take the path on the other side passing to the left of the wooden garage. Follow the paling fence steeply uphill to reach a road by St Clares and Cobwebs. Turn right for just over 100yd.

9) Then, opposite the drive to Assisi, go left into woodland. Keep right at a fork and follow the path to join a drive at Coombe Farm.

10) Turn left and continue along the drive to reach a road. Turn right and walk to the junction with Hammer Lane.

11) There, take the path on the left. Cross a stream and immediately turn right to return to the road at the pumping station. From there, retrace the outward route to the start.

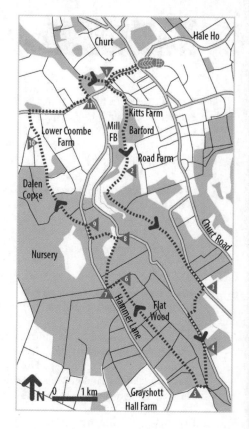

Clandon Park

START At TQ044512, the church of St Peter and St Paul, West Clandon GU4 7RG

DISTANCE 4 miles (6.5km)

SUMMARY An easy walk with views of the gentler slopes of the North Downs

PARKING Free parking at nearby Clandon House

MAPS OS Sheets Landranger 186; Explorer 145

WHERE TO EAT AND DRINK The Horse and Groom, www.horseandgroommerrow.co.uk. Open daily from 12:00

Clandon Park, www.nationaltrust.org.uk/clandon-park. Available during House opening times

A varied and level walk featuring a golf course, open fields, woodland, residential developments and a stately home.

① From the lych gate of the church, take the path between the cottages opposite to join a grassy lane. When you reach the far end of the field, turn left on the path and follow the driveway. Stay on this as it goes through the Clandon Regis golf course and around the back of the clubhouse to return to the main road.

② Continue ahead beside White Lodge and then cross a track going through a metal gate. Maintain the same direction at the end of the fields, crossing a stream by way of the footbridge. Please note that the lake up to the left here is private. After just under ¾ mile through the fields and a further metal gate, enter woodlands for a short step until you reach a residential road.

③ Turn left opposite the house Ridge Way. Pass Henchley Dene on your right.

④ Turn left to take the surfaced path running parallel to the road. This path leads you under the main road through a tunnel. Bear left and walk along a series of pathways and alleyways through an estate of houses to eventually pass some allotments on your right.

5 Turn left into Merrow Street, where the church of St John the Evangelist is visible ahead. Turn left along Epsom Road to reach a roundabout.

6 Enter the grounds of Clandon Park by going to the left of the left lodge. After about ¼ mile, leave the drive by bearing left at a fingerpost. The path leads across fields, recrossing a track beyond the farm buildings of Temple Court. Enter woodland and cross a bridge over a pond. From the bridge you can clearly see Clandon House, and glimpse the Ionic Temple dating from 1838 and comprising six columns surmounted by a cupola. Continue on the track to reach the main road (the A247).

7 Turn right along the road to return to the church.

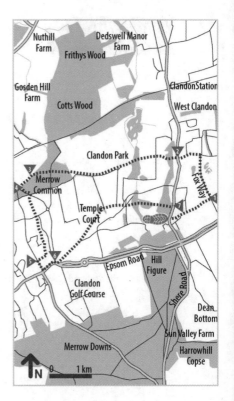

Points of interest

Clandon House – The house, and part of Clandon Park, has been administered by the National Trust since 1956. Built in the early 1730s, the property has distinct Italian features as influenced by the Venetian architect Giacomo Leoni. Inside, the Marble Hall is considered to be one of the country's best examples of an 18th century interior. There are also good collections of porcelain and furniture, and the museum of the Queen's Royal Surrey Regiment.

The grounds were laid out by Capability Brown around 1770, and within the Park is Temple Court, the residence and working farm of the Earl of Onslow.

Colley Hill

Start At TQ263523, the car park off Wray Lane at the top of Reigate Hill, RH2 9RP

Distance 4 miles (6.5km)

Summary A moderate walk along level well-made tracks but with a steep chalky descent and ascent

Parking In the car park at the start

Maps OS Sheets Landranger 187; Explorer 146

Where to eat and drink Urban Kitchen, Reigate Hill, www.urbankitchen.co.uk

The Yew Tree, Reigate Hill, www.theyewtreereigate.co.uk

A walk along the top and foot of the North Downs with a stiff climb towards the end!

1 Leave the car parking area by ascending to reach and cross the white-painted footbridge. Continue on the track, the North Downs Way, to reach a crossing. Keep ahead here, going past the two masts. In just under ½ mile, you will come to a broad expanse of grassland, at the start of which there is a 12-pillared shelter.

2 Continue along the track to reach a tower dated 1911 and inscribed 'Sutton District Water Company'.

3 Here, bear left to walk on the grass in order to enjoy the fine views to the south, but continue walking in the same direction. Further on, the North Downs Way is rejoined at a National Trust sign for 'Colley Hill'. Continue ahead passing a Coal Tax post on the right.

4 Then reaching a roadway by Swiss Cottage, turn left. Go left again beyond the gates of Mole Place, following the path between two metal posts. Ahead now is a steep, but shady, descent. Continue to a path crossing, where the route leaves the North Downs Way.

5 Turn sharp left through the barrier and stay on the path which lies just above field level, ignoring all side tracks. At a fork, take the

right stepped path. Continue, going past a paddock, to reach a residential road close to another National Trust sign, this one for 'Pilgrims Way'.

6 Walk up the road to the hill crest and there bear half-left up the bridleway which runs up the left side of a brick wall.

7 The bridleway leads to the main road (the A217). The Yew Tree is about 75yd down the road to the right. Turn left and go along the pavement for 80yd.

8 Take the bridleway to begin the stiff climb up to a path junction near the masts passed on the outward journey.

9 Turn right and after a few steps look left through the gap to see the London skyline.

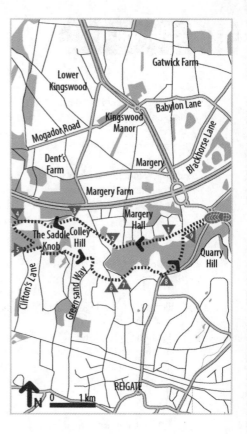

When ready, reverse the outward route back to the start.

Points of interest

12-pillared shelter – This shelter was presented to the Borough of Reigate by a Lt Col R.W. Inglis, and bears the date 1909. From its seats there is a fine view of the sweep of the North Downs.

Compton

START At SU956469, the Harrow Inn, Compton, GU3 1EG

DISTANCE 4 miles (6.5km)

SUMMARY Moderate walking along country lanes and through woods and fields

PARKING Limited roadside parking

MAPS OS Sheets Landranger 186; Explorer 145

WHERE TO EAT AND DRINK The Harrow, www.theharrowcompton. com. Open daily 11:00–23:00; Sunday 12:00–2230

The Tea Shop at Watts Gallery, www. wattsgallery.org.uk/tea-shop. Open daily 10:30–17:00. Closed Mondays apart from Bank Holidays

The Withies Inn, www.thewithiesinn. com. Open daily from 12:00; restaurant closed Sunday evenings

A walk around the village of Compton, famous for the Watts Gallery.

1 With the pub on your left, follow the road in the direction of the A3, passing the church of St Nicholas. At Down Lane, turn right, following the sign to 'Watts Gallery', and walking past the cemetery. At Coneycroft Farm, continue along the road to visit the Watts Gallery. Return to the farm from the Gallery.

2 Take the public footpath between the fencing and leading to a white-painted barn. Pass through the gate and turn right at the barn to follow the public footpath sign along the driveway. At the end of the drive, go through a gate and turn left along the footpath.

3 Continue ahead and at the end of the path, by a garden, go down the steps into a gully and turn right to reach a lane and the entrance to Little Polsted. Continue along to pass Polsted Manor.

4 After just over ¼ mile and at the grass triangle junction, turn left to reach the Withies Inn, and continue to reach the New Pond Road crossing.

5 Go ahead along The Avenue.

6 After 150yd, turn right along a bridleway. Cross a diagonal footpath

and bear left at the metal gate at the end of a drive. Walk between a mixed garden hedge and a hedgerow to join a track alongside a field.

⑦ Turn right at the field's first corner.

⑧ Then turn left when confronted with a fine sweep of grassland. Go uphill with the grassland on your right to reach some trees. Enter the woods and climb the steps.

⑨ Keep walking along an alleyway leading to a residential road.

⑩ Here, turn right into Mark Way and continue on the road for just less than ½ mile.

⑪ At the end of the road, turn right onto a bridleway and at the gates to Broomfield Manor keep ahead and take the path in front when you reach the Foxhanger Down entrance.

⑫ At the edge of woodland, bear left through a kissing gate and continue for 600yd until you reach a stile in the corner of the field.

⑬ Diagonally cross the next field towards the left of the farm barns.

⑭ Cross another stile and proceed past the barns and down.

⑮ Go over a concrete stile to reach a path that leads directly to The Harrow and the start of the walk.

Points of interest

Watts Gallery – A purpose-built art gallery created for the display of works by the Victorian artist George Frederic Watts. Over 100 paintings by G.F. Watts are on permanent display at Watts Gallery, spanning a period of 70 years.

The Devil's Punch Bowl

START At SU891358, National Trust car park, GU26 6AE

DISTANCE 4 miles (6.5km)

SUMMARY A moderate walk with a steep ascent at the end

PARKING In the car park at the start

MAPS OS Sheets Landranger 186; Explorer 133

WHERE TO EAT AND DRINK National Trust café, Hindhead. www. nationaltrust.org.uk/hindhead-and-devils-punchbowl/eating-and-shopping

A stunning walk with massive views, cute cottages and pretty streams.

1 From the rear of the car park, walk past the notice board to reach the viewpoint. At the foot of the steps in front of the viewpoint, take the upper left path. At the post, keep ahead beside the paling fence to reach a seat placed at a spot where there is a magnificent view. Shortly the walk reaches the 'Highcombe Edge' sign, by the electricity sub-station.

2 Take the bridleway, which passes through a cattle grid and gate and follow the line of poles to reach a bench seat on the left. Just beyond, there is a three-way fork.

3 Take the right path to see the memorial, and then carry on to rejoin the track. After a gradual descent, a right hairpin bend is reached.

4 Go around this bend and proceed downhill.

5 Near the bottom, by a gate at the corner of a field, turn left to pass above Keeper's Cottage. The track descends to a stream, which is crossed by a bridge. Climb up on the other side and turn left along a path.

6 Now do a clockwise loop to reach a track.

7 Turn right here. Go past a seat with the inscribed details of Peter Schessers's activities and shortly afterwards, cross a cattle grid.

8 Keep straight ahead to pass Gnome Cottage, and continue to a junction near to the Youth Hostel.

9 Turn left, going around and beyond Highcombe Farmhouse.

10 Bear right just after the bend at the marker post and yellow salt box. Now follow the Roam 639 route for a little over ½ mile to reach a steep incline with some steps.

11 At the top of the steps, turn right and continue for a short distance to return to the start.

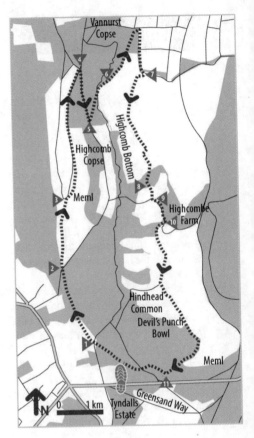

Points of interest

The Devil's Punch Bowl – A large natural amphitheatre and beauty spot, is now a walker's paradise after the building of the Hindhead tunnel and the re-routing of the A3. The main road that used to skirt the area has been replaced by a broad grassy walkway sown with heather and planted with 200,000 new trees and shrubs as part of a National Trust restoration project.

Ewhurst Green

Start At TQ094394, Ewhurst Cricket Club

Distance 4 miles (6.5km)

Summary Easy level walking through paddocks, grassland and woods

Parking On the road at the start

Maps OS Sheets Landranger 187; Explorer 134

Where to eat and drink Nothing en route, but the nearby village of Ewhurst has an excellent village shop

A pleasant stroll around the countryside between Ewhurst Green and Cranleigh, 'the largest village in England'.

1 Cross the main road and take the footpath to the right of Willow Cottage. Cross a stile and go into a field, and keep ahead to enter woodland. Cross the stile at the edge of the woodland, and turn left. After 50yd, go left through a gate. Continue along the path.

2 Turn right at a T-junction, to join a bridleway.

3 After 400yd, at a crossroads, turn right. At the end of the path go through a gate, and walk past the yew hedge of Old House. Pass a concealed pond on your right.

4 Turn left joining a footpath. Keep ahead through a wooden gate and keep the hedgerow close to your left. Just before a wooden five-bar gate, turn left though a metal gate, then immediately turn right along a footpath entering woodland. Cross a stile and keep ahead to walk through open grassland heading for the distant trees. Now, maintain direction through a series of fields, gates, stiles and woodland until you cross a footbridge with metal poles.

5 Cross the grassland ahead and re-enter woods.

6 Just before a metal gate, turn right onto a bridleway and look out for sightings of Pitch Hill in the distance. Ignore a footpath on the

right and continue, climbing and bearing around to the right.

⑦ Pass Wanborough House and as you descend, take a footpath on the right with three steps. At a meeting of paths, keep straight ahead walking parallel to the houses. Just past these, drop down, cross a plank bridge, and reach a driveway.

⑧ Turn right for 50yd, then left following the footpath.

⑨ You now proceed on a broad track through an area of beech trees, gorse bushes and the occasional Christmas tree. At the edge of more woodland, cross a stile to enter a paddock. Cross a track and several more paddocks with rustic pole fencing. Go over a bridge and stile combination and go through a five-bar gate to join a drive.

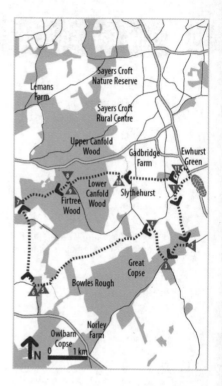

⑩ Turn left along the drive and rejoin the footpath, passing behind a stable to exit through another gate. Go straight ahead on the wide grassy track.

⑪ At the end of the track, turn left onto a tarmac drive and follow it to the main road. Turn right to return to the start.

Points of interest

Ewhurst Cricket Club – Founded around 1847, it was awarded The Best Kept Cricket Ground in Surrey in 1996. More recently, in 2010, the club won the Village Cricket League Knockout Cup.

Oaks Park and Little Woodcote

START At TQ275612, Oaks Park Tea
Rooms, off Croydon Lane (A2022),
SM7 3BA

DISTANCE 4 miles (6.5km)

SUMMARY An easy and level walk on
a variety of terrain

PARKING Car park at the start

MAPS OS Sheets Landranger 187;
Explorer 161

WHERE TO EAT AND DRINK Oaks Park
Tea Rooms, Banstead

A walk of mixed interest, a highlight being the outstanding lavender field at
the end (best visited during summer months).

1 With the café to your right, take the drive signposted to the right-
hand car park and proceed through the barrier. Go downhill for ¼ mile
following the line of trees to reach a road. Turn right and cross over.

2 Walk up the concrete track into the Little Woodcote Estate.

3 At the crossing, turn right to reach the Carlshalton Campus
building on the left and a road.

4 Cross the road and take the public bridleway signposted to 'Little
Woodcote Lane'.

5 At the next road, cross to Dell Cottage and turn left up the pathway
under the trees to reach the drive to New Lodge Farm.

6 Turn in the drive and walk along the dead-straight avenue of trees
to the bend.

7 Go over the stile ahead. More stiles follow on this grassy path,
bringing you to a road.

8 Turn right passing the golf clubhouse. Follow the tarmac bridleway
beside the course and the car park to the beginning of the Clockhouse
estate.

⑨ There, turn right and 150yd past the Jack and Jill pub, take the track to the right of the road.

⑩ Beyond the spiked gate, proceed along the left path to reach a track, from where there is a view to the skyscrapers of Canary Wharf, the City and Central London.

⑪ Keep ahead beside the trees for around 450yd to reach a chalky track. Cross and walk about 35yd down the path beyond this.

⑫ Turn left through a narrow metal K barrier and walk across rough grassland. At the top, bear right to reach a road. Turn left and, with great care, walk to the '30mph' sign by Hylands Nurseries.

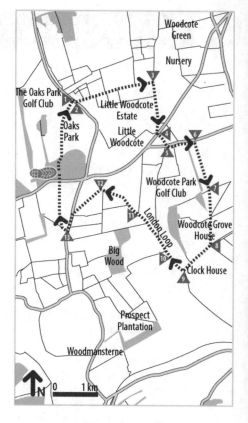

⑬ Turn right over a stile and go diagonally across the meadow beyond. The following field is the site of Mayfield Lavender, a wonderful treat at the end of this walk. Cross the road to return to the start.

Points of interest

Oaks Park – During June, at nearby Epsom racecourse, The Oaks and The Derby are run. The former is named after the estate that occupied the site of today's park. The latter is named after the twelfth Earl of Derby who organized races here.

Shere and Gomshall

START At TQ073480, Shere village car park, GU5 9HF

DISTANCE 4 miles (6.5km)

SUMMARY A moderate walk on chalky tracks and some well-made trails

PARKING Free parking in the village car park

MAPS OS Sheets Landranger 187; Explorer 145

WHERE TO EAT AND DRINK Dabbling Duck, www.thedabblingduck. uk.com. Open daily from 09:00

Shere Delights, www. sheredelights.co.uk. Open daily 09:00–18:00

The William Bray, www. thewilliambray.co.uk. Open daily 11:00–23:00

A lovely walk up to and along part of the North Downs Way and through the pretty village of Shere.

① From the car park, turn right and follow the track keeping the recreation ground on your right. Pass under the A25, taking great care underfoot in the dark tunnel, and climb steadily uphill staying on the main chalky and flint path. At the top there is a concrete reservoir to your left; this is a relic of the Second World War as are the numerous pill boxes in this area of Surrey.

② Turn right at this junction onto the North Downs Way. Follow this well-made track for just under 1 mile to reach Gravelhill Gate. Here, at a five-way junction, you will find another reservoir.

③ Turn right, following the signpost to Gomshall and begin a pleasant shady descent to Cole Kitchen Farm, nestling in the fold of the hills. The drive beyond joins a road which leads down to Gomshall.

④ Turn left along the main road to reach Gomshall Mill.

⑤ Turn right to cross the bridge. Follow the road past the football and recreation grounds, and at the railway arch keep right to continue along the main road.

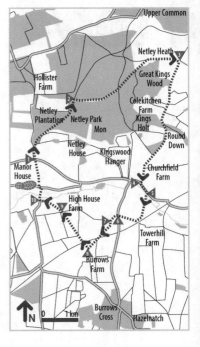

6 At a junction by the bus shelter, cross Queen Street and continue along Gravel Pits Lane.

7 Take the left trail at Gravel Pits Farmhouse, passing the tennis court, and cross the railway bridge. Now, make your way along the right side of the field.

8 Turn right through the barriers and back over the railway. The following paths point you towards Shere church, with a panoramic view of the North Downs. At the next junction take the path that leads you to the church.

9 Walk along the road with the church to your right and pretty cottages to your left.

10 Turn right at the square and cross the river to go along Middle Street. At the end, set in the wall, is the Drinking Fountain. Bear left into Upper Street for a few yards, then turn right to reach the start of the walk.

Points of interest

Shere – A pretty village with a central cluster of old village houses, shops including a blacksmith, tea house, art gallery, two pubs and a Norman church.

The Drinking Fountain in Shere – The small fountain was given to the village in 1886 by two maiden ladies who lived locally. They were very religious and saw alcohol as the devil. They wanted visitors to the nearby White Horse Pub to have an alternative 'local' drink and thought water was a good option.

Thursley

START At SU900398, car park near the cricket pitch, GU8 6QA

DISTANCE 4 miles (6.5km)

SUMMARY An easy walk

PARKING Free parking at the start

MAPS OS Sheets Landranger 186; Explorer 133 and 145

WHERE TO EAT AND DRINK The Three Horseshoes, www. threehorseshoesthursley.com. Open daily 12:00–15:00; 17:30–23:00

A charming walk featuring chocolate box cottages and fairytale glades.

1 From the car park turn left onto the road and at the triangle of grass with its village sign depicting Thor. Go right along The Street to the church of St Michael and All Angels.

2 Just up from the churchyard gates, take the footpath over the stone steps, and bear left around Hill Farm. At the end of some fields, take the right fork and drop down to the Smallbrook buildings.

3 Turn left up a lane, keeping ahead at the bend and following the Greensand Way (GW).

4 Follow the path to the left and until you reach Hedge Farm.

5 Turn right at the road, but go only as far as the bend.

6 Here, turn right onto a footpath and skirt two fields before going down into a picturesque glade with a small stream flowing under a canopy of trees. Cross the stream and climb a slope, passing Ridgeway Farm at the top. Walk forwards and down to reach a junction.

7 Continue ahead up Hyde Lane.

8 About 120yd after the pond at Upper Ridgeway Farm, turn right down a track which will bring you to Little Pitch.

⑨ There, turn left along a road.

⑩ Having passed the last bungalow, March Hares, turn right through a line of tree stumps. Continue forwards and upwards until a wide sandy track with telegraph lines above.

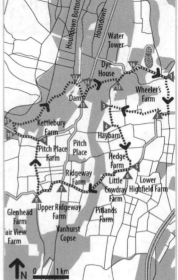

⑪ Turn right onto the track. After around 200yd keep a look out for a steep narrow path on the left. It is worth the short climb through the heather to reach a triangulation pillar for a spectacular view and will only take a few minutes. Return to the sandy track and turn left. Ignore a left fork under power lines and descend gently under the pines. Turn right to cross a fenced bridge.

⑫ Take the narrow path between the roadway and Hounmere House and follow it up to a road.

⑬ Turn left for 100yd.

⑭ Go right onto a footpath that guides you to a rustic bridge. Descend through a gully to reach a picturesque stream.

⑮ Cross a stile and turn left along the drive ahead to reach a road. Walk uphill between cottages to reach a bend.

⑯ Turn right here and take the gully path straight ahead. This path rejoins the road by the cricket pitch and the start of the walk.

Points of interest

Thursley – The village was probably originally a site where the god Thor was worshipped. A rock near the village is often called Thor's Stone. The small parish church has a finely carved Anglo-Saxon font and two Anglo-Saxon windows in the chancel. In the churchyard there is the gravestone of the Unknown Sailor, murdered nearby in 1786.

Virginia Water

START At SU981688, the car park beside the Wheatsheaf Hotel, GU25 4QF

DISTANCE 4 miles (6.5km)

SUMMARY Easy walking on well-made paths

PARKING Plenty of parking available in dedicated car park

MAPS OS Sheets Landranger 175; Explorer 160

WHERE TO EAT AND DRINK The Wheatsheaf Hotel, www. chefandbrewer.com/pub/ wheatsheaf-hotel-virginia-water/ c4306. A good selection of quality pub food at pub chain prices; served daily from 12:00–22:00 and 12:00–21:30 on Sunday

A pretty walk around the lake passing through wonderful gardens and a visit to a totem pole!

1 From the car park make for the lakeside path via the modern café, picnic area and toilets, and turn left. After 150yd take the left fork to descend to the foot of a waterfall. Until now the route has been roughly parallel to the A30; it now heads away from the road, following the lake shore towards the remains brought from the Roman city of Leptus Magna, visible over to the left. Originally the remains were located near Tripoli in Libya, but in 1818 they were brought to England, and were erected here in 1827 at the direction of George IV.

2 Continuing along the shore, the Frost Farm Plantation is passed on the left. It comprises mainly oak, beech, sweet chestnut and hornbeam, and has a thriving population of toadstools and insects. Before reaching the graceful, five-arched bridge, the route passes the pink Blacknest Gate Lodge, built in 1834.

3 The route continues along a straight drive, eventually curving around to cross another arm of the lake.

4 Just beyond, take the path following the pointer to the 'Valley Gardens'. This area provides a feast of colour, being planted with a great range of rhododendrons, camellias, magnolias and other trees,

shrubs and herbaceous plants which have been selected and planted with the aim of producing year-round colour and interest.

⑤ After an ascent, turn right at the junction and follow the sign for 'Totem Pole ½ mile'.

⑥ The Totem Pole was presented to the Queen by the Canadian province of British Columbia to commemorate its centenary in 1958. From here it is about ½ mile of walking back to the start.

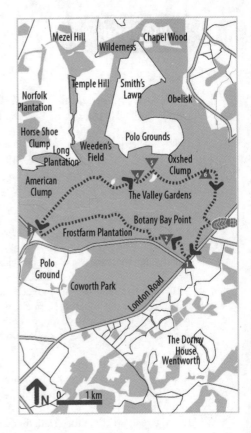

Points of interest

Virginia Water – Lying within Windsor Great Park, part of it is in Surrey and the remainder is in Berkshire. It is an artificial lake and was made in 1746 by damming and by the diversion of several streams. In recent years, the shores of the lake have been used for scenes in the Harry Potter films and for the boat scenes in *Robin Hood*.

START At TQ118381, The Scarlet
Arms, Walliswood RH5 5RG

DISTANCE 4 miles (6.5km)

SUMMARY An easy level walk with 11
stiles!

PARKING Village car park opposite
the pub

MAPS OS Sheets Landranger 187;
Explorer 134

WHERE TO EAT AND DRINK The Scarlett
Arms, www.scarlettarms.co.uk.
Open daily from 12:00–15:00,
18:00–23:30 Tuesday to Thursday;
12:00–23:30 Friday and Saturday;
12:00–21:30 Sunday and 18:00–
22:00 on Mondays

A walk through charming woodland and fields in a peaceful setting.

1 Turn left from the car park to reach the red phone box. Turn left
again and follow the fingerpost straight ahead. Cross a plank bridge
and go through a gate, pass through another gate to come into a field
and go through the gardens of Walliswood Farm. Exit via the stile.

2 Turn right onto the road.

3 At The Pheasantry turn right onto the Byway.

4 At the road junction, turn right following the public footpath up a
private drive passing Lyefield House.

5 At the gate, take the public footpath over the stile on the left and
cross the field diagonally towards the trees and the hedge. Cross the
stile and follow the path around to the left.

6 At the end of the path cross the stile and continue down the gravel
drive with the spectacular view of the Surrey Hills.

7 Turn left onto the bridleway.

8 After just over ¼ mile and at the junction with a 4-way signpost,
take the public footpath on the right crossing over a stile and entering a
field. Head straight across the field to the gate. Pass through the gate and

keep straight ahead aiming for the stile in the corner. Cross the stile and go ahead keeping to the left of the field with the hedge on your left.

9 After around 100yd and at a ditch, turn right and follow the path, keeping the embankment on your right and follow the field down. Go down some steps and across a wooden bridge with two stiles. Head up to a field, cross the field exiting by a metal gate to reach the road.

10 Turn left then immediately right onto a public footpath. Cross two stiles and a field. Keep the hedge on your right to reach another stile in the corner, go straight through. Cross over the stream.

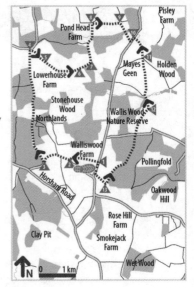

11 At the junction with the Byway, go straight ahead to pass a golf course on your left. Continue for a further 175yd.

12 Take the footpath on your right just before the buildings. Go through the gate and keep to the left, follow until you reach a road. Cross and go straight ahead into the woods. Keep ahead at a junction going towards some houses. Go straight over a driveway keeping metal railings on your left. Cross the drive and keep straight ahead passing a pretty thatched cottage on your right. Continue over the footbridge and up some wooden steps.

13 At the junction at the back of some houses, turn right. Continue until you reach the road. Here, turn right to return to the start.

Points of interest

Wallis Wood – Two words, unlike the village name, Wallis Wood is a Surrey Wildlife Trust nature reserve just north of the village. It is home to the rare triangle spider which lives in yew trees and is only recorded in one other site in Surrey. Dormice and the extremely rare Bechstein's bat are also inhabitants.

START At TQ227553, Mere Pond,
Walton-on-the-Hill KT20 7UE

DISTANCE 4 miles (6.5km)

SUMMARY An easy walk through
woods, grassland and along a golf
course

PARKING Plenty of parking available
on the road

MAPS OS Sheets Landranger 187;
Explorer 146

WHERE TO EAT AND DRINK The
Sportsman, www.
thesportsmanmogador.co.uk.
Hearty traditional pub grub,
burgers and jacket potatoes at
reasonable prices. Serving food
daily from 12:00–23:00; Sundays
12:00–22:30

A pleasant stroll through woodland and wide open spaces and a walk
alongside one of the world's top 100 golf courses.

1 Begin the walk by going down Deans Lane opposite the pond
for 125yd. Take the public bridleway on the left and at the crossroads
take the middle path. Walk to the busy B2032, at the top of a dip with
wooden barriers. Cross the road with care.

2 Head across the grass in the direction of the masts on the skyline,
which are located at the top of Reigate Hill. At a fork, bear right
following the public bridleway sign. The spire of St Andrew's church,
Kingswood, which has been prominent to your left, disappears behind
a clump of trees as you approach the woodland and bear down a wide
grass track to reach the bottom corner.

3 At the bottom of the grassy slope, as you enter the woodland, there
is a four-way wooden signpost on the right. Take the public bridleway
straight ahead. Keep to the bridleway ignoring the path to the left with
the wooden barriers until you reach the end of a lane at Hogden Cottage.

4 Turn right at the bridleway just before the Coal Tax post and keep
ahead as the path rises to pass a line of Leylandii conifers obscuring
the view of the substantial house The Red Lodge. At the bottom of its
garden, go ahead to the far end of a field.

⑤ At the junction with the gap in the trees, go straight ahead keeping the woodland close on your left.

⑥ Eventually, you will see a metal pole barrier, close to which is The Sportsman. Go almost to the end of the road.

⑦ Then turn right along a bridleway.

⑧ Just before the path crosses an arm of the golf course, turn right at another Coal Tax post shortly after a notice board. It is now a straight walk back, with the famous golf course always to your immediate left, and several more Posts as well as a mini-pond to look out for. Recross the B2032 by the entrance to Walton House.

⑨ Take the footpath which leads back to the start of the walk.

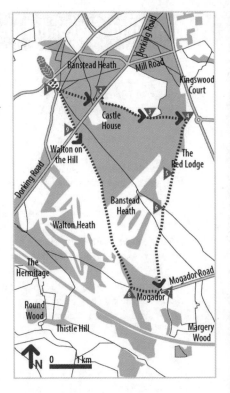

Points of interest

Coal Tax Post – The white Coal Tax Posts, or Boundary Marks, are reminders that the Corporation of the City of London had the right up until 1890, to levy a duty on coal brought into the City. This duty helped to pay for the rebuilding of several churches damaged in the Great Fire of 1666. After an Act of Parliament passed in 1861, the area for collection of duty was enlarged and over 200 posts were erected. The ones seen on this walk bear this date and the name of the Regents Canal Ironworks. Other marking refer to the indexation of 'The London Coal and Wine Continuance Act, 1861', which was passed in the 24th/25th year of Queen Victoria's reign.

Around Hascombe and Hascombe Hill

START At TQ002394, The White Horse Inn, Hascombe GU8 4JA

DISTANCE 4¼ miles (6.75km)

SUMMARY Hard with some difficult terrain but magnificent views

PARKING White Horse Inn car park

MAPS OS Sheets Landranger 186; Explorer 133 and 145

WHERE TO EAT AND DRINK The White Horse Inn, www.whitehorsepub.net. Open daily from 11:00, seven days a week. Lunch from 12:00 and dinner from 19:00, serving good food at a fair price

A difficult walk with steep climbs and uneven paths, incorporating fields and forestry and some beautiful trails around Hascombe.

① From the inn, cross the road and follow the fingerpost past the metal posts to the gate and grass beyond; you are now on the Greensand Way. Go through the gate, climb to the wood. Fork right after another gate and right again after a short stiff climb. At the crest, keep ahead past the public footpath sign.

② Now leaving the Greensand Way, follow the wide track ahead for around 700yd, passing deforestation on the right, to a T-junction.

③ Turn right. Keep on the broad track.

④ After ¼ mile admire the view from the bench on your left.

⑤ Continue on the track as it forks to the right downhill.

⑥ Rejoin the Greensand Way to the right.

⑦ Continue along the bridleway for ½ mile to reach the top of a tricky descent. Take care as you go down.

⑧ Bear left joining a lane near Hoe Farm. At the end of the lane is Hascombe village and fountain.

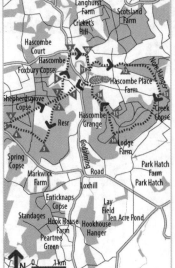

⑨ Take the footpath opposite and cross the stream. Shortly after, turn right heading for the houses ahead.

⑩ Upon reaching the houses, turn right rejoining the Greensand Way and catch sight of St Peter's church.

⑪ Before reaching the church or the nearby pond, turn left at the school house up a bridleway. After climbing for roughly ½ mile, ignore a left fork leading to overhead lines.

⑫ A level, muddy section follows at the top of the further ascent; keep right joining a path from the left.

⑬ At the end of the field, continue half-right ahead, ascending steeply through woodland to reach the upper slopes of Hascombe Hill with magnificent views. Ignore paths to the right, and keep on the rhododendron path along the ridge.

⑭ Proceed clockwise around the hill until you reach an area with a large elevated log bench. Take the path behind the bench, turn right after 100yd then immediately left at a large log chair. Continue along the path.

⑮ At a fork lower down go right on the upper, narrower path.

⑯ Bear right down a gully. At the end of the gully turn left down the lane to reach the White Horse.

Points of interest

Dunsfold Aerodrome – Built by soldiers from the First Canadian Army in 1942, the site has recorded a number of milestones: in May 1953, Neville Duke broke the world speed record sound barrier at an average speed of 727.63mph in a prototype Hunter Mk3. In October 1960, the first tethered flight of the forerunner of the Harrier Jump jet took place leading to its first conventional flight a month later.

Banstead Wood and Kingswood

START At TQ273583, the car park at the foot of Holly Lane, CR5 3NR

DISTANCE 4¼ miles (6.75km) or 6 miles (9.5km)

SUMMARY Easy walking through woods and farmland and on smart residential streets

PARKING In the car park at the start

MAPS OS Sheets Landranger 187; Explorer 146

WHERE TO EAT AND DRINK The Kingswood Arms, Kingswood, www.kingswoodarms.co.uk

Pleasant valley views are enjoyed on this varied and undemanding walk.

1 From the rear of the car park, take the path up to the fingerpost at the opening to the woods. Head towards Perrotts Farm but immediately take the left path along the fenceline. Follow for just over ¾ mile and at a gate and fingerpost, bear right towards Banstead Woods. After 200yd, a path comes in acutely from the left.

2 25yd beyond, the short and long walks divide beside a prominent yew tree. The shorter walk continues ahead for 250yd to a T-junction.

3 Go left following the Banstead Countryside Walk. Stay on this path as it curves around and emerges from the woods.

4 Cross the stile into grassland, keeping to the right to reach a brick barn at Perrotts Farm, and rejoin the longer walk.

The longer walk drops steeply down under the yew and emerges onto Fames Rough. Head for the bottom where there is a gate leading you under a railway arch.

3 Turn right to enter an area run by the Woodland Trust. At the far end, turn left.

4 After 25yd, go right to a residential road. Turn right at the junction, and continue as far as Copper Birch.

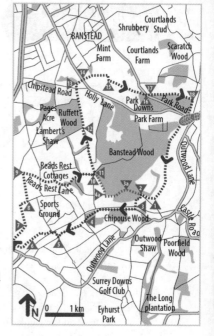

5   Take the path down right and cross the railway track. Go left, cross a car park and walk along the driveway/private road that joins St Monica's Road.

6   Keep ahead to a junction. The Kingswood Arms is to the left. Continue to the top of Furze Hill.

7   Turn left at the office complex entrance. At the junction with Copt Hill and Doric Drive, turn right for 100yd.

8   Go left along a footpath that leads to a bridleway.

9   Turn right. Keep ahead for around ½ mile to a farmhouse.

10   Here you rejoin the shorter walk.

11   Take the first footpath on the left after the walks rejoin. A gateway with a stile follows.

12   Go through a copse and veer to the right walking downhill beside a field. Keep ahead after one stile and cross another.

13   Turn right along a narrow path.

14   Cross the main road and go up the footpath opposite.

15   Skirt a field and follow the footpath towards Park Road. Cross two broad tracks.

16   100yd beyond, veer left to cross a road.

17   The path opposite forks left downhill.

18   At a fence at the bottom, turn right to return to the start.

Bocketts Farm

START At TQ167562, Leatherhead parish church KT22 8BD

DISTANCE 4¼ miles (6.75km)

SUMMARY Easy riverside and trail walking

PARKING On street parking is available by the church

MAPS OS Sheets Landranger 187; Explorer 146

WHERE TO EAT AND DRINK Old Barn Tearooms, Bocketts Farm, www.bockettsfarm.co.uk. Open daily from 1:00–17:30 serving well priced traditional cakes, lunches and cream teas

An interesting walk along the River Mole and the surrounding area of Bocketts Farm.

1 From Park Gardens in front of the parish church of St Mary and St Nicholas, go along the main road away from the town centre to reach Thorncroft Drive on the right. Turn into it, soon crossing the River Mole. Walk past Thorncroft Manor beyond which a crossing is reached.

2 Turn left here, following the public footpath sign to Norbury Park. Go under the bridge, which carries the by-pass towards Guildford, and continue through the picnic area. At the end of the picnic area, continue ahead, going through a gate. Walk over the hill crest ahead and drop down to reach another gate. Go through and follow the track on the far right with the trees immediately to your right to reach a secluded cottage.

3 Turn right and pass through a gate, walk under a railway bridge. Continue along ahead and upwards for just under ½ mile until you reach a drive.

4 Turn right here and keep going to pass Norbury Park House on your left. At a large junction with an information board and some benches, keep straight ahead and go through a wooden barrier passing a sawmill on the left.

5 Shortly, turn right onto a public bridleway. Stay on the main track

ignoring the turn for 'Walnut Tree Clump' on the right, and descend.

⑥ At the junction turn right onto a public bridleway.

⑦ Turn right at the crossroads in about 300yd and head towards Bocketts Farm. At the farm, keep ahead on the concrete track to reach the main road (A246).

⑧ Cross the road with great care and continue along the bridleway opposite.

⑨ At the junction signposted to 'Gimcrack Hill' at the waterworks turn right and follow the track down and round to the left to cross the railway line. Continue ahead and soon the outward route is rejoined, follow it to return to the start.

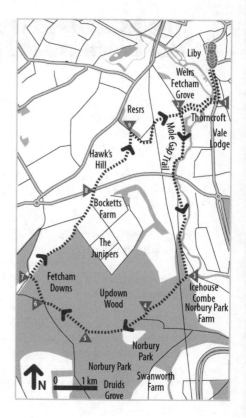

Points of interest

Bocketts Farm – Bocketts Farm is a working family farm with animals and play areas, aimed at children's entertainment and education. The 18th Century Old Barn Tearooms serves homemade cakes and cream teas, hot homemade lunches, all day English breakfasts, sandwiches and ploughman's.

Ockley and Vann Lake

Start At TQ148402, The Inn on the Green, Ockley RH5 5TD

Distance 4¼ miles (6.75km)

Summary A moderate walk with views to Leith Hill and a visit to a nature reserve

Parking In the lay-by opposite the pub or in the nearby village car park

Maps OS Sheets Landranger 187; Explorer 134 and 146

Where to eat and drink The Inn on the Green, www.inn-onthegreen. co.uk. Food served daily 12:00–14:30 and 18:30–21:30; Saturday 12:00–21:30; Sunday 12:00–20:00

A varied and interesting walk, but the terrain can be difficult at times with tree roots and some steep inclines.

1 Turn left at the green metal fingerpost 50yd from The Inn on the Green and take the footpath which ascends to a field. Keep to the right side of this as far as the crest. At the top of the field you can see a white house and barn conversion ahead and a gap in the trees to the left. Cross the field bearing left and pass under some power cables between two wooden telegraph poles. Head for a rusty metal gate in the left corner at the edge of some woodland.

2 Go through the gate and follow the track beyond to a bridge. Take care as you climb the slope on the other side comprised of rocks and old bricks, ignoring a path off to the right.

3 At the field corner at the top, take the path in front. This continues around a garden and then joins a road at the entrance to Weavers.

4 Turn right along the road and after roughly 700yd pass Stylehurst Farm.

5 Soon after, turn right into Vann Lake Road. You will soon reach the Blue Ridges Mobile Home Park. Continue ahead passing Lake House on your left and Herons March on your right.

6 After a few yards you will come to some steps tucked into the bushes

which lead you down to Vann Lake. At the dam, face the lake and take the steps on your right to take you back to the lane.

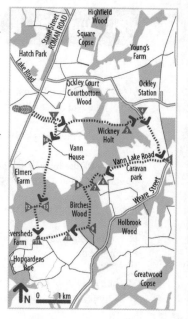

⑦ Turn right down the lane to reach Rill Cottage.

⑧ Just past the wooden shed lower down in the garden, turn left onto a bridleway. Stay on this bridleway, passing a wooden sign for Candy's Copse on your right and eventually you will come to a crossing path. Here, there is another Candy's Copse sign on the corner to your right.

⑨ Turn right at this junction and continue through the woods until you come to a field ahead. Turn right again and keep going straight with the path taking you past the woods on your right, and soon turning to fields, heading for Eversheds Farm.

⑩ Just before the Atcost barn, cross the stile on the right and aim for the far left corner. Cross the stile and descend gradually in the woodland and cross a wooden bridge with tubular railings. Bear left up the steep slope beyond to reach a crossing.

⑪ Turn right up the cart track.

⑫ Bearing left after 100yd into woodland. Keep ahead to reach a field gate and a stile.

⑬ Go straight ahead, ignoring the stile and footpath on the right, for ¼ mile, heading for the line of houses in the distance. Cross a stile and continue to the far right corner where there is another stile at the back of a garden.

⑭ Cross this stile onto a track and then cross a drive to follow the path to the top of a field. There, keep left to cross a stile after 100yd. Halfway along the second field you will rejoin the outward route: now reverse the outward route back to the start.

Runnymede

START At SU996718, Cooper's Hill car park, Englefield Green TW20 0LB

DISTANCE 4¼ miles (6.75km)

SUMMARY Moderate walking through woods, fields and along the river

PARKING Public car park at the start

MAPS OS Sheets Landranger 176; Explorer 160

WHERE TO EAT AND DRINK Italian Concept, www.italianconcept restaurant.net. Open daily 09:30–21:00, Fri and Sat till 22:00, Sun 10:30–17:00. Closed Mondays except Bank Holidays

Magna Carta Tearoom, www. nationaltrust.org.uk/runnymede/ eating-and-shopping/. Open daily 09:00–17:00

Starting and finishing at the top of a hill, this riverside and woodland walk visits three memorials to major historical events.

① The Air Forces Memorial is only a short distance along the road from the car park where the walk begins. Having visited it (no dogs allowed), continue on the road, around the bend to a T-junction and turn left here, through the gate by the National Trust sign for Cooper's Hill Slopes. Several flights of steps will take you down through woodland. At the bottom of the steps, continue ahead passing through two gates. The walk continues to the right to reach Langham Pond.

② Note that the public footpath directs you straight for around 275yd before you head to the right across the water meadow. At Langham Pond, stop for a while to read the information board.

③ Then take the wooden path to the other side of the pond. Continue on, passing through a gate.

④ Turn left at a meeting of paths. Cross the concrete bridge shortly after another gate and go straight across heading towards a line of houses facing the A30 in the distance.

⑤ Just before reaching the road, turn left along a footpath to the A308,

Windsor Road. Cross the road and continue along Yard Mead to reach the riverbank.

⑥ Turn left. After a pleasant riverside walk of about a mile, you reach a road.

⑦ Turn right and cross the road. Head for the Magna Carta Monument.

⑧ Next, turn right and continue along until you reach a steep cobbled granite path leading to the John F. Kennedy Memorial.

⑨ Continue on the path rising to the left behind the inscribed stone to join a drive that skirts the private grounds of Brunel University to meet a road.

⑩ Cross over to the safety of a footpath and turn left and follow the road to the crest.

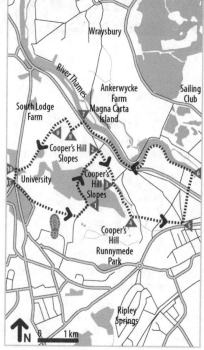

⑪ Go left again into Coopers Hill Lane to return to the start.

Points of interest

Air Forces Memorial – This memorial commemorates more than 20,000 air personnel killed in the Second World War who have no known grave. Their names are inscribed along the sides of the grass quadrangle.

Runnymede – This is the site where King John signed the Magna Carta in 1215. The monument was erected by the American Bar Association in 1957 and takes the form of a rotunda with eight columns, covering a stone inscribed 'To commemorate Magna Carta symbol of freedom under law'.

Brockham and Betchworth

Start At TQ197496, Brockham
Green, RH3 7JN

Distance 4½ miles (7.25km)

Summary An easy walk near the
River Mole

Parking On the road at the start

Maps OS Sheets Landranger 187;
Explorer 146

Where to eat and drink The Dolphin,
www.dolphinbetchworth.com. Food
served daily from 12:00–15:00 and
18:00–21:00; Saturday 12:00–21:00
and Sunday 12:00–2:000

The Grumpy Mole, www.
thegrumpymole.plus.com/
brockham. Food served daily from
12:00–21:00; 12:00–20:30 Sunday

Some stunning views and impressive properties are enjoyed on this circular,
gentle terrain walk.

① From Brockham village green, walk to the far side of the church. Turn
left into Wheelers Lane and continue along for ¼ mile. Opposite a hedge
and between Four Way House and Wheelwrights, there is a footpath
marked by a stone at ground level.

② Turn left on this path, go through a gate, and follow the edges of
several fields. Go through a metal gate and cross the field heading towards
the woods.

③ At the end of the wood there is another metal gate. Go through this,
and continue through the field to reach a thicket, keeping this on your left
side.

④ When a corner is reached, enter a copse via a metal gate and continue,
crossing over a wooden bridge and exiting into a field. Cross the field to a
road beside a bridge.

⑤ Turn left and continue to Betchworth and The Dolphin.

⑥ Turn right down Wonham Lane. Pass the junction with Sandy Lane,
to the left, and continue to Wonham Manor.

⑦ Just beyond, on the left is bridleway; go through the gate, keep to the left and follow this, climbing upwards for around 350yd.

⑧ Turn left over a stile. Follow alongside a brick wall and pass a house on your left. Keep going until you come to a metal gate. Go through and down some steps to reach a road. Turn left.

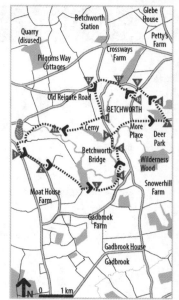

⑨ 40yd further on go left again at Sandy Lane. Pass the entrance to Hartsfield Manor.

⑩ 75yd further down the hill, turn right opposite the public footpath sign. Take some steps up the grassy slope, and cross a drive. Go through the field and follow a path. At the end of the path, cross a drive and continue to walk between fencing.

⑪ When a road is reached turn left. At the junction with The Street, bear right, and at Station Road, keep left.

⑫ After 150yd, turn left down a footpath opposite the Post Office.

⑬ At the bottom of the footpath, turn right into The Walled Garden. Keep the cultivated field on your right, with at first a high hedge and a line of impressive chestnut trees on your left. Continue along the path, through a wooden gate.

⑭ Pass some back gardens to reach a track. Go down left and cross the River Mole. The surfaced path ahead leads you back to Brockham.

Points of interest

Brockham – The village green is the site of one of Surrey's most famous annual bonfire night celebrations. Around £20,000 is raised for local organizations and good causes each year.

Hydon Heath and Hascombe

START At SU979402, Hydon's Ball car park off Salt Lane, GU8 4BB

MAPS OS Sheets Landranger 186; Explorer 133, 134 and 145

DISTANCE 4½ miles (7.25km) or 6 miles (9.5km)

WHERE TO EAT AND DRINK The White Horse, Hascombe, www. whitehorsepub.net

SUMMARY The shorter walk provides easy walking; the longer walk has a couple of steep climbs

Winkworth Arboretum, Godalming, www.nationaltrust.org.uk

A walk mostly through woodland, visiting the pretty village of Hascombe.

① From the car park, walk along Salt Lane for 50yd. Turn left, then right down the stony track. Continue around the bend to a fork.

② Take the track right uphill, and continue ahead at the crest. After an area of grassland, the track beyond rises to reach a drive.

③ Turn right at the top of the drive to the entrance to Winkworth Arboretum. In the car park, take the footpath to the right of the gate, with fencing to your left. At a road, turn right for 200yd.

④ Turn left onto the Sundown bridleway, following telegraph poles.

⑤ At the junction, bear left towards Winkworth Hill.

⑥ Just before Sullingstead, bear right beside the ivy-clad wall and continue down a path to a road. Cross the road and go through a gate.

⑦ At a T-junction, turn right. At another green gate, keep ahead for about 100yd then cross a stile on the left.

⑧ Head diagonally right across a field and over a stile to join a path by a shed. Here, the two walks separate. For the shorter walk, turn right to reach the road, turn right again, then left into Mare Lane and walk for ¾ mile to a junction. Turn right into Markwick Lane at ⑧a. 100yd later at

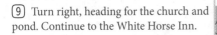, before the Hydon Heath roadsign, take the left bridleway. Continue, ignoring side paths. When you reach a plank seat at (10a), rejoin the longer walk. For the longer walk, go left to a drive.

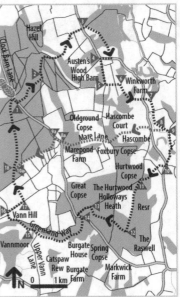

⑨ Turn right, heading for the church and pond. Continue to the White Horse Inn.

⑩ Cross the road and follow the fingerpost to the gate. Go through the gate, climb to the wood and fork right after another gate and right again after a short climb. Keep ahead leaving the Greensand Way.

⑪ Follow the wide track for around 700yd to a T-junction.

⑫ Turn right. Keep on the broad track and after ¼ mile pass a bench on your left. The track curves around to the right.

⑬ Go left, rejoining the Greensand Way and down to a road. Go left for 100yd.

⑭ Then turn right along a bridleway. In just under ¾ mile, the path meets a lane.

⑮ Continue to the junction where the Greensand Way turns left, but you do not. Instead, walk towards Maple Bungalow.

⑯ Turn right past the gate to ascend on the sandy track.

⑰ Turn left at the first bridleway towards the trees. At the junction beyond the belt of trees, rejoin the shorter walk by the plank seat.

⑱ With the seat behind you, go forward and climb for a few yards to join a higher track marked with an 'Octavia Hill Trail' post. Turn right onto the broad track, keeping ahead and leaving the marked trail. Pass the NT 'Hydon's Ball' sign on your left and continue to return to the start.

START At TQ224469, The Plough
RH2 8NJ

DISTANCE 4½ miles (7.25km)

SUMMARY An easy level field walk

PARKING On street parking at the
start

MAPS OS Sheets Landranger 187;
Explorer 146

WHERE TO EAT AND DRINK The Plough,
www.theploughleigh.com. Proper
pub grub in a traditional setting.
Open daily 11:00–23:00; Sundays
12:00–22:00

The Three Horseshoes, www.
thethreehorseshoes-pub.co.uk.
Light bites and more substantial
dishes available in this friendly pub.
Open daily 12:00–23:00; Sunday
12:00–20:00

A circular walk around the picture postcard village of Leigh.

1 From the pump opposite the pub, walk past the church. Just beyond the entrance to Willow Cottage, take the path through the gate and cross the field diagonally. In the next field, cross the ditch on the left, using a stile to reach a road. Cross the road and continue along the track opposite, beside Hillview Farmhouse, through four fields.

2 After the fourth, cross a stile and turn right beside a hedgerow. Follow the yellow arrowheads and pass through two metal gates reaching a path through trees. Go through another gate and stile to a road.

3 Turn left and pass the entrances of Moon Hall College, Burys Court School and Little Flanchford Farm.

4 On the right by the pole 20yd past the farm drive, cross the stile in the hedgerow and follow the bank to a wooden bridge.

5 Follow the river upstream to join a concrete drive, then turn left along the drive.

6 Fork left at the end of a brick building. The drive continues beyond double gates, then deteriorates to a stony track.

[7] Stay on the track, bearing left to join a tree-lined drive.

[8] At a 3-way fingerpost, within sight of a small bridge, turn right. Leave the drive and aim for the gap in the hedge. Cross a plank bridge and the following two fields diagonally, and continue towards a red house.

[9] At Tamworth Cottage, cross the drive to enter the farmyard, continuing along the track to a field. Pass the wooden fencing on the right, keeping ahead for the crest and a stile in the hedgerow.

[10] Go over the stile and bear right down the side of the next field, walking beside the trees. Go diagonally left across further fields to exit through a wooden gate in the bottom left corner.

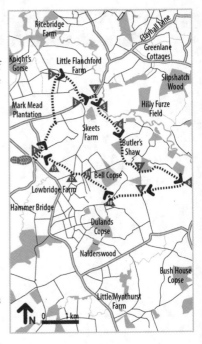

[11] Walk forward to join a wide bridleway. Follow for 25yd then cross planks and a stile on the right.

[12] Turn left, walk around the edge of the field reaching the far left corner. Turn left over a stile and go right to the hedgerow.

[13] Cross a wooden bridge. Beyond the next field, an alley leads into the churchyard and returns you to the start.

Points of interest

Leigh – The village name is pronounced 'lie'. The pretty St Bartholomew's church has memorial plaques and a stained glass window commemorating members of the Charrington family of brewing fame, who lived in Burys Court, which is passed on the walk. On the village green there is a History Box, a converted red telephone box that houses photos and information about the village.

Newdigate and Capel

START At TQ198420, St Peter's church, Newdigate RH5 5AW

DISTANCE 4½ miles (7.25km)

SUMMARY Easy level walking on a mixture of terrain

PARKING Some parking is available in the car park behind the pub

MAPS Explorer 146

WHERE TO EAT AND DRINK The Crown Inn, www.thecrowncapel.com. Open for drinks daily 12:00–23:00; Sunday 12:00–21:30. Food served Tuesday to Saturday 17:30–23:00; Sunday 12:00–15:00

The Six Bells, www.sixbells-newdigate.co.uk. Open daily from 12:00–23:00; Sunday 12:00–21:00. Food served Monday–Thursday 12:00–15:00, 18:00–21:00; Friday–Saturday 12:00–21:00; Sunday 12:00–19:00

A gentle walk between two villages.

1 Walk down the street towards Rusper for 100yd, then take the footpath beside the last house on the right. Keep ahead through two fields using the gates; in the third field, ignore the first public footpath on your right and continue round the bend to the 4-way signpost.

2 Turn right and continue straight ahead in this field to cross a drive. Carry on into the next field keeping alongside the wood on the right.

3 In the bottom corner, shortly after a plank bridge, turn right at the stile and signpost. Pass through the copse and emerge into a clearing, follow a line of electricity poles to reach another plank bridge and a stile. Cross and keep left along the next field.

4 Cross into the adjacent field at the end corner and keep ahead to reach a road at Mizbrook Farm. Turn left.

5 At the bend go right at Mizbrook Yard. Keep left along the drive skirting two paddocks. Continue to the back of some houses.

6 Cross a bridge over a stream to enter a recreation ground, then leave by going to the right of the pavilion at the top.

7 Turn left along the main street of Capel to reach the church of St John the Baptist and the Crown Inn. Continue through the village to a small green.

8 Turn left. Pass through a gate and walk along the left hedgerow to enter the adjacent field. Walk to the crest and take a path through the meadow beyond to reach the far hedgerow.

9 Cross the plank bridge and, keeping the trees on your left, follow the path for 70yd until the line of trees falls away.

10 Pick up the path in the large field and go diagonally across to a well-hidden metal gate. Go through to enter a wood and keep ahead on the bridleway to a cottage and the road beyond.

11 Turn right and continue for 150yd to reach Temple Mead.

12 Turn left and after a few yards go right at the brick pillars to enter a field that runs parallel to the drive. Keep left and continue ahead.

13 When you reach the tennis court, turn left.

14 Then turn right shortly after. Cross the following two fields keeping just to the right of the central hedgerow. A raised path takes you through some woods to reach a bridge. Cross the bridge and 75yd further on cross a stile on your left. Then cross a stream.

15 Keep left and climb to reach a stile in the corner, cross and head for the farm buildings.

16 In the farmyard, turn right in front of the brick barn to pass a pond. Go ahead over two stiles and through the lower gate to reach a road. Turn left along the road to return to the church.

Tadworth and Headley

START At TQ231562, Tadworth
Station, KT20 5SP

DISTANCE 4½ miles (7.25km)

SUMMARY An easy mixed terrain
walk , with some gentle inclines and
descents

PARKING Plenty of on-road parking
near the station, restrictions in place
Monday to Friday 08:00 to 09:30

MAPS OS Sheets Landranger 187;
Explorer 146

WHERE TO EAT AND DRINK The Chalet
Bakery, www.thechaletbakery.
co.uk. 5 mins walk from the start,
open daily 08:00–16:00, Saturday
08:00–14:00, closed Sunday

The Chequers Inn, www.
chequerspub.co.uk. Moderately
priced food and drinks served all
day from 12:00

The Cock Inn, Headley, www.
cockinnheadley.com. Open from
11:00 for good food and drink at
reasonable prices

A gently undulating circular walk with some interesting features and views.

① Turn left from the station and head for Barclays Bank, turn right here
and walk up the path to reach a road. Go right for a few yards then turn
left on to a bridleway opposite Spindlewoods.

② Take the track signposted to 'Mere Pond'. At the pond, cross the road
and go down Deans Lane, which brings you to the Riddell Memorial Hall.
Turn right into Meadow Walk, at its end continue along a footpath to
enter the churchyard of the Parish Church of St Peter the Apostle.

③ Beyond the lych gate, cross the green to the left and proceed along
Chequers Lane. Just after the bend, turn right into Queens Close and
continue ahead, going through posts. At the end of the paddock beyond
the lawn of Walton Manor Farm, go through a gate on the left and walk
ahead for 20yd turning right beyond a fence. The M25 is now in front of
you, and in the distance you can see Wembley Stadium.

④ Leave the field and follow the barbed wire fencing round to the right,
with the spire of Headley church straight ahead. Descend beyond a gate to
reach a stile hidden in the bushes.

⑤ Go along a path going left, which takes you under the motorway. Gently ascend on the track next to woodland, then turn left and head for the farm buildings.

⑥ About halfway to them, at the fingerpost, go right over a stile to reach the end of the field. Turn right at the metal fingerpost and walk through the fields to the church, close to which is the Headley Hills Restaurant & Bar.

⑦ At the lych gate, turn right and descend to enter woodland. Continue to a track, and turn left, pass under the motorway again. Continue downhill and after just under ¼ mile, keep left to skirt a paddock on your right.

⑧ Climb to reach a road and turn right. At the junction beyond the Hurst Road nameboard, bear left.

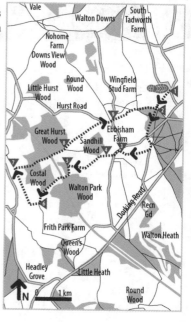

⑨ After a few yards, turn right along a footpath beside 'Pilgrims'. At the end, pass the barrier by a Coal Tax Post and fork left through the woods to rejoin the outward route just before Spindlewoods, returning to the station along the same alley followed on the outward journey.

Points of interest

The Arch of Wembley Stadium – At 133 metres tall and 315 metres long, the arch is the longest single roof structure in the world. The design ensures that there are no pillars that may obscure the view of the spectators.

Coal Tax Post – Up until 1890, the Corporation of the City of London had the right to levy a duty on coal brought into the City. This duty helped to pay for the rebuilding of several churches damaged in the Great Fire of 1666. Over 200 posts were erected after an Act of Parliament was passed in 1861.

Tilford and Frensham Little Pond

START At SU873435, Tilford village green, GU10 2BU

DISTANCE 4½ miles (7.25km)

SUMMARY An easy level walk through woods and by the River Wey

PARKING Free parking around the green or in the car park

MAPS OS Sheets Landranger 186; Explorer 145

WHERE TO EAT AND DRINK The Tern Cafe, www.nationaltrust.org.uk/frensham-little-pond. Open Thursday–Sunday 1:000–15:00, serving snacks, homemade sandwiches and cakes

The Barley Mow Inn, www.thebarleymowtilford.com. A typical country pub serving traditional food. Open: Summer 11:00–23:00; winter 11:00–15:00, 18:00–23:00

An interesting walk incorporating a farm renovation project, a beautiful lake and a pretty section of the River Wey.

☐1 With your back to the Barley Mow Inn, turn right to reach the corner of the Green and cross to reach a short gravel track. Beyond the gate to the Malt House, veer left, then immediately go right, down a grassy path to a wooden gate. Continue ahead through woodland to meet the River Wey and eventually pass through another gate.

☐2 When the path joins a wide track, turn right, and after a few yards take the left branch at a path fork.

☐3 Just past the last house, go ahead, leaving the track which turns left into private land.

☐4 When a kissing gate is reached, go through and turn right along a sandy bridleway. After around ½ mile, the route continues here by turning right, but first do enjoy a leisurely stroll, and perhaps some refreshment, around the shores of Frensham Little Pond which is just across the road ahead.

☐5 Back on the route, the path to the right goes past a cottage and then crosses the River Wey on a footbridge. Pass through Pierrepont Farm and keep right through a gate. Now follow a path that offers a pleasant walk through the forest to join a track leading out on to a road.

6 Cross straight over the road to reach a path opposite and follow this to reach another road.

7 Cross the road and follow Sheephatch Lane opposite, following it to a bridge.

8 Just over the bridge, take the path going up and right. Stay ahead on this path, ignoring the crossing track, until it meets a surfaced lane. Keep going to pass an impressive house on the left.

9 At the end of the stone wall, turn off right down a footpath and follow it to reach a road. Go right along the road, crossing over the River Wey again to reach the start of the walk on Tilford Green.

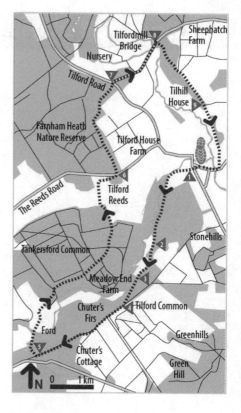

Points of interest

Pierrepont Farm – This dairy farm of over 200 acres was gifted to the Countryside Restoration Trust in 2006. As well as extensive pasture, the farm has wooded areas and a wet meadow next to the River Wey, which has been designated an SSSI (Site of Special Scientific Interest) because of its important flora. A new state-of-the-art dairy has just been built, improving the welfare of the pedigree Jersey herd.

Albury and Blackheath

Start At TQ048478, Albury Post Office, Albury GU5 9AG

Maps OS Sheets Landranger 186; Explorer 145

Distance 4¾ miles (7.75km)

Summary Moderate walking on a mixture of terrain

Parking On-street parking available at the start

Where to eat and drink The Drummond Arms, www. thedrummondarms.co.uk. An attractive pub specializing in homemade pies. Open daily from 12:00–23:00; Sunday 12:00–22:30

With only the occasional train to break the silence, there is plenty of stunning scenery to enjoy throughout this walk.

1 Walk up Church Lane and continue up Blackheath Lane. At the crest, take the bridleway to the left.

2 After 300yd take the right fork, continue along the path with trees to the left and field to the right. Go through a weighted gate to a field. Follow the path straight ahead, down and across the railway. Take the sunken avenue between the trees past a cottage.

3 Go past converted barns curving around to a T-junction.

4 Turn right, taking a bridleway up a small valley.

5 At a junction marked by a '237' post, walk ahead up the raised narrower path forking slightly right taking you through an area of bracken and trees.

6 Turn left when the path meets a wider track.

7 At a junction with a triangle of grass, keep the triangle to your right and go straight ahead.

8 At the crossroads, continue ahead aiming for the tall pine trees. Stay on the path all the way through the trees. At a junction with two blue-

topped posts, take the path leading from the post on the right. On exiting the trees at a multiple junction, go straight ahead through two sets of wooden barriers.

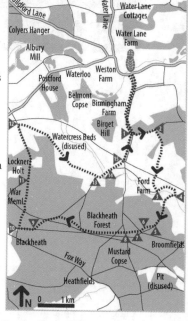

⑨ At a third set, turn second right towards a car park. From the car park, take the bridleway on the right for 100yd, joining a road to pass electrical equipment on your right. At the end of the road turn left.

⑩ Then take the narrow Downs Link path on your right between fence panels and a beech hedge.

⑪ Continue about ½ mile to reach white gates and a Lodge just before the railway bridge.

⑫ Turn across the drive and enter the field to the right of the Lodge, follow the undulating footpath past an impressive house on your right. Keep going to cross a stile. Go down the surfaced track past stables and across a stream.

⑬ Walk up to another stable block, at the back of which cross a stile into the field on the left.

⑭ Go diagonally up to the top right corner.

⑮ Cross the railway and continue up the side of the next field to reach a stile just before the Dutch barn. Turn left on the lane, retracing your outward route to the start.

Points of interest

Albury – A small village in an Area of Outstanding Natural Beauty. Many of the houses feature chimneys attributable to the architect Augustus Pugin, one of the designers of the Houses of Parliament.

Basingstoke Canal and Brookwood Cemetery

START At SU946559, Pirbright Green pond, GU24 0JU

DISTANCE 4¾ miles (7.75km)

SUMMARY An easy walk on level ground

PARKING On street parking available at the start

MAPS OS Sheets Landranger 186; Explorer 145

WHERE TO EAT AND DRINK The Cricketers Inn, Pirbright. www. cricketersinn.yolasite.com. The White Hart, Pirbright. www. thewhitehartpirbright.co.uk

A varied walk taking in a section of the Basingstoke Canal and the famous Victorian Brookwood Cemetery – NO DOGS ALLOWED.

1 With the pond on your right, walk along the lane to The White Hart. Cross the main road and continue along Church Lane. At the end of the church wall, turn right along a footpath. When the path reaches a road, turn left for around 250yd.

2 Then go right along Vapery Lane.

3 Near the end, just past the bungalow called Twin Oaks, bear right along a path skirting Goal Farm and Pirbright Golf Course to reach a road.

4 Cross the road and walk through a tunnel under the railway.

5 At Cowshot Bridge turn right along the towpath of the Basingstoke Canal. Stay on the towpath for 1½ miles, crossing to the other bank at Pirbright Bridge to reach the busy Bagshot Road beside a petrol station.

6 Turn right, go across at the traffic lights and walk under the railway bridge.

7 Now turn right along Cemetery Pales for 400yd to reach the entrance to Brookwood Cemetery.

8 Turn in left and follow the drive to the St Edward Orthodox Church, dedicated to the martyr who died in 979 at Corfe in Dorset.

9 Take the St David's Avenue opposite.

10 Bear left at the fork by the Columbarium.

11 At the junction by the Bent memorial, turn right and go either way around the semi-circle. Follow the straight track ahead, going across a surfaced avenue by the St Alban shelter, to reach its far end. Go ahead on a narrow path into woodland, then bear half-right on a wide track which meets a lane beyond a pole barrier.

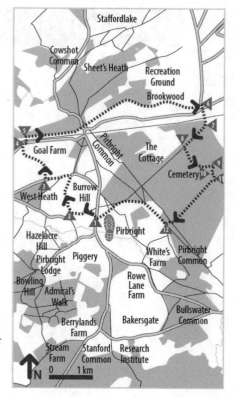

12 Turn right to join a residential road, Chapel Lane. This leads to the main road and Pirbright Green where the walk started.

Points of interest

Brookwood Cemetery – At a time when the capital was finding it difficult to accommodate its increasing population, Brookwood Cemetery was founded in 1852 by the London Necropolis and National Mausoleum Company to provide a final resting place for London's dead. The site was sold to the Commonwealth War Graves Commission in the 1920s to accommodate Commonwealth victims of the First World War.

Dormansland and Dry Hill

START At TQ404422, Dormansland Post Office, RH7 6PY

DISTANCE 4¾ miles (7.75km) or 6½ miles (10.5km)

SUMMARY A moderate undulating walk on decent terrain

PARKING Plenty of street parking at the start

MAPS OS Sheets Landranger 187; Explorer 147

WHERE TO EAT AND DRINK The Plough Inn, Dormansland, www. ploughdormansland.com

Fine views across four counties are enjoyed on this hilly walk.

1 Walk down the High Street and Plough Road to reach The Plough Inn. There, turn right into Ford Manor Road.

2 At the fork, bear right towards Greathed Manor. Follow the drive for just over ½ mile.

3 Then fork left onto the bridleway. Go left and continue, passing farm buildings and a house, to enter some woodland on a rough trail.

4 Emerge from the wood through a gate into open countryside to reach Littleworth Cottage at the crest of a hill.

5 Descend for 50yd to the first bend. Turn right through the metal gate, then fork left at the next. A steady ascent now brings you to the first of a cluster of houses. Turn right at the T-junction to reach the end of the paddock.

6 For the shorter walk, follow the path right until you reach Old Lodge Farm, where you rejoin the longer walk. For the longer walk, turn left, climbing steadily to gain impressive views to both the front and behind. Beyond the East Surrey Water compound there is a trig pillar; this is the site of Dry Hill Fort, the ramparts still visible to the right.

7 The obvious descent line now leads around Beeches Farm and down

a lane past Woodlands House to within 75yd of a road junction. Look out for a footpath sign and a gate on the right.

8 Take the path across a field and through another gate into a wood. Cross a bridge and a stile and follow the path across the next field until you reach a wooden gate with a yellow footpath arrowhead. This leads to the drive of Lower Stonehurst Farm.

9 At the farm continue ahead and slightly right, passing a bungalow and both wood and brick built stables. A gentle ascent through pasture will now bring you to Upper Stonehurst Farm. Follow the drive into the dip.

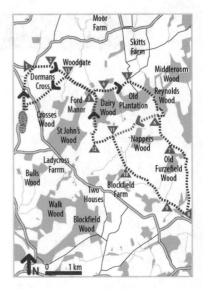

10 Then turn off right through a field and wood to reach a path that climbs up to Old Lodge Farm on the top of a ridge.

11 There, turn left on the road, rejoining the shorter walk. Just before Burnt Pit Farm, turn right through the wooden gate, going past a barn.

12 Continue downhill, bearing to the right to enter woodland. An easy descent now reaches the outwards route close to Home Farm. Reverse the route past the entrance to Greathed Manor, going as far as the stone pillars.

13 Now turn left beyond the lodge and walk to the second road crossing. There, turn left to return to the start.

Points of interest

Greathed Manor – Built in 1816, Greathed Manor is now a nursing home. During wartime it served as a hospital for service men. Between the wars it witnessed frequent visits by the royal family, who were invited for picnics and tennis.

Grayswood and Gibbet Hill

Start At SU917346, Grayswood village green, GU27 2DN

Distance 4¾ miles (7.75km)

Summary A hard walk with some steep inclines

Parking On-street parking at the start

Maps OS Sheets Landranger 186; Explorer 133

Where to eat and drink The Wheatsheaf, Grayswood, www. thewheatsheafgrayswood.co.uk

A strenuous walk up the second highest hill in Surrey and around the pretty area of Grayswood.

1 Head to the church and walk down the road for 100yd. Turn left along a public bridleway towards Damson Cottage Farm. Pass through a railway arch and veer right beyond the gates.

2 Keep on the drive to Damson Cottage Farm itself, and walk around the house to enter woodland.

3 The path soon ascends. Cross a broad track and keep ahead to reach a crossroads.

4 Turn left and walk up the wide sandy track to a T-junction.

5 Go right and continue to a bend.

6 Here, go left and bear left again 15yd later for a short steep climb.

7 At the junction at the top of the climb, go to the marker post and follow the bridleway, keeping an old concrete plinth on your left. Continue to pass a high metal gate. Keep ahead to reach a junction.

8 Turn right to soon reach a 5-way junction with a barrier.

9 Go straight ahead for an optional ascent to the top of Gibbet Hill.

When ready, return to the 5-way junction. With Gibbet Hill behind you, go right, then left downhill passing through a gate.

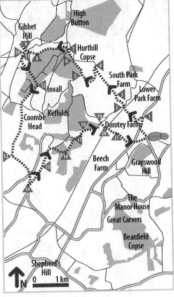

(10) At the first fork, take the lower path that swings left.

(11) Keep on this path dropping down through a clearing and to go through a wooden gate. Pass a pond on your left, and continue to a fork.

(12) Bear right and keep ahead to emerge from woodland and reach a road.

(13) Turn left and follow the road to reach Inval House. Cross the road beyond and climb to the crest of the hill.

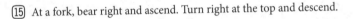

(14) Double back left on the road, then take the bridleway on the left that runs parallel to the road.

(15) At a fork, bear right and ascend. Turn right at the top and descend.

(16) Bear left to reach a metal post with a yellow top. Go ahead to reach metal gate posts, then a small wooden gate, turning right before a house.

(17) Walk around the edge of the field keeping the house and fencing on your left. Go through a kissing gate and continue down a gully.

(18) Walk past a small lake on the left, and descend to cross a rivulet. Climb briefly to reach a crossing and take the marked footpath on the right.

(19) Follow the path to the railway line and use the steps to cross with great care.

(20) At the white gate, go right to cross a stream on a wooden footbridge.

(21) Continue up more steps and along the path to reach a drive. Turn left and at the main road cross straight over to follow the path back to the start.

Start At TQ425518, the Carpenters Arms, Limpsfield Chart, RH8 0TG

Distance 4¾ miles (7.75km)

Summary Medium walking on undulating and mixed terrain

Parking On the road at the start

Maps OS Sheets Landranger 187; Explorer 147

Where to eat and drink The Carpenters Arms, Limpsfield Chart, www.carpenterslimpsfield.co.uk

① Take the path behind the bus shelter and cross the road. Continue towards The High and turn right in front of the house down to Quince House. Follow the path beside the wall to reach a lane. Turn left, passing Caxton House to Chartlands Farm. Go down the track beyond the gate.

② At the bottom of the slope, go over the stile on the left and bear right to cross the rising slope of the field to reach another stile. Cross and go right, heading for the corner of the field.

③ Cross the stile and turn right towards the buildings leaving the field at the entrance to The Old Lodge.

④ Pass the pond and continue past Moat Farm Cottage, keeping ahead until you come to a footpath under overhead lines.

⑤ Turn right and walk to a farm drive beyond a bridge. Turn right to a pond, turn left at the garden gate. Follow the path around paddocks and between a hedgerow. Cross a stile and climb a hill to the top left corner.

⑥ Cross the stile in the corner and climb up the path beside a fence.

⑦ Near the top, go through a tall wooden gate with yellow footpath arrowheads until you reach a 4-way fingerpost.

⑧ Go down the road to a bend.

⑨ Before Oast Cottage take the footpath on the right. Go through a gate to the road at Pains Hill Chapel.

[10] Turn right and walk to the main road. Cross to reach Ridlands Lane, and turn left along a bridleway.

[11] Bear left after a few yards and bear left again further down to cross two fairways of a golf course.

[12] Turn right off the track, keeping the trees to your left. Walk past the green.

[13] Then follow the path for 200yd to a gate leading into a field on the left.

[14] Halfway down, opposite a gate, turn right into a wood and, on emerging, cross a field strip.

[15] Enter more woodland and continue along the edge for 600yd.

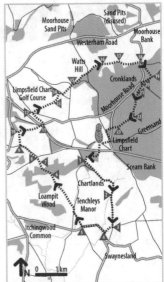

[16] Go through a latched gate and head for a similar gate opposite.

[17] After roughly 100yd, take a path to the right to Moorhouse Car Park.

[18] Go through the car park and cross the road. Walk along a track, passing High Chart and at a marker post, turn right to enter a wood.

[19] Turn right at the T-junction along the sunken path to approach a gate and a road. Turn left away from the gate.

[20] Then go right after a few yards to once again enter a conifer wood.

[21] After 150yd and at a post, follow the yellow arrowheads left to reach a junction by the Askew memorial seat.

[22] Take the path behind the seat and over the wooden walkway to pass a pond. Fork left beyond this, rising to join a broad track.

[23] Go right along the track, keeping ahead at the NT arrow. Bear left at the next fork to a car parking area. Cross the road to the cricket pitch and turn left to a junction. The starting point is to the right.

START At TQ193706, Kingston Gate car park, KT2 5LD

DISTANCE 4¾ miles (7.75km)

SUMMARY Easy walking along the well-made trails of Richmond Park

PARKING In the car park at the start

MAPS OS Sheets Landranger 176; Explorer 161

WHERE TO EAT AND DRINK Pembroke Lodge Tea Rooms, Richmond Park, www.pembroke-lodge.co.uk

Deep into the park, you can enjoy complete tranquillity but with plenty of deer to keep you company.

1 From the exit at the top of the car park, cross the road and head up and into the oak trees. At the top, and when you emerge onto open grass, bear left. Walk past the enclosure of trees known as Kings Clump, and keep ahead to reach the drive of the white privately owned royal residence Thatched House Lodge.

2 Cross the drive and fork right passing the chicken wire and wooden rail fencing of the house next door. Follow a wide path through bracken and go across a small bridge with brick parapets and fork left to reach a horse-ride.

3 Continue across on a level path through the middle of the grassland to reach the fenced Isabella Plantation.

4 Enter the plantation through the main entrance, near to the bus stop at Bottom Gate, going through a pretty iron gate and, after having explored, leave by a similar looking entrance, Broomfield Hill Gate, at the far end.

5 Turn left and walk around the boundary fence. Further round, the walk reaches a locked gate that is part of the plantation but does not provide public access. Fork half-right and drop down to the horse-ride. Go forward to reach a paved roadway and keep going to reach the Pen Ponds.

6 Walk along the causeway between the two ponds.

7 At the end, turn left, then fork half-right. Keep ahead over the next horse-ride to reach the perimeter road by Oak Lodge. Cross over to the right and go through the car park to enter the grounds of Pembroke Lodge.

8 At the back of the house, turn left and walk through the gardens. Exit by a gravel path leading off the bend and pass through a metal gate to enjoy wonderful views towards Kingston-upon-Thames.

9 Take any of the paths running parallel to the road, then descend into a little valley just up from Ham Gate. Follow the track inside the boundary wall to eventually return to the start.

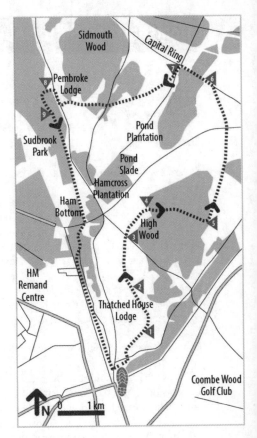

Points of interest

Isabella Plantation – Planted in the 1830s, the Isabella Plantation is best known for its evergreen azaleas, which line the ponds and streams, and are at their peak of flower in late April and early May. The plantation is also home to large collections of rhododendrons and camellias, and other rare trees and shrubs.

Gomshall and Sutton Abinger

START At TQ089478, Gomshall station, GU5 9NY

DISTANCE 4¾ miles (7.75km)

SUMMARY A moderate walk with a few inclines

PARKING Free at Gomshall station

MAPS OS Sheets Landranger 187; Explorer 145 and 146

WHERE TO EAT AND DRINK Tillings Café, www.tillingscafe.co.uk. Open daily 09:00–17:00; weekends 09:00–17:30

Gomshall Mill, www.homecountiespubs.co.uk/gomshallmill. Serving premium priced traditional food daily from 12:00–21:30 and till 21:00 on Sundays

The Volunteer Inn, www.volunteer-dorking.co.uk. A real ale pub serving hearty pub grub at restaurant prices. Food served daily from 12:00–14:30; Monday and Tuesday 18:30 –21:00; Wednesday to Friday 18:30–21:30; Saturday 12:00–21:00 and Sunday 12:00–15:00

An open-country walk with good views of the North Downs.

1 Leave the station through the gateway on the Guildford-bound side and walk down to a road. Turn left, and a few yards after the Tillingbourne Trout Farm, turn left again into a public byway.

2 After 200yd, go right up a narrow public footpath that leads into Piney Copse, an area of woodland.

3 Follow the path marked National Cycle Network route 22 and go through another gate. Walking alongside open grassland and parallel to the North Downs, enter the Abinger Roughs via a gate. After ¼ mile and an ascent, you will come to a triangle of open grassland.

4 Pass the National Cycle Network route 22 marker post and take the sharp right here to reach a gate after 50 yards. Go through the gate and take the path running along the upper side of the field beyond. Go through another gate and descend through a gully to reach the main A25 road. Cross the road with great care and continue along the bridleway/

concrete driveway opposite. Pass between the houses of Paddington Farm and ascend on a public bridleway. At the top, 75 yards beyond a pole carrying overhead lines on your right you will come to a junction with a double-trunked oak tree.

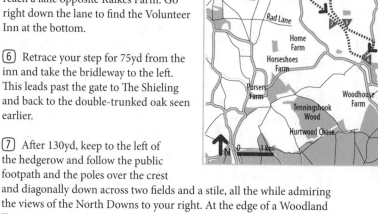

5 Turn left here and take the public footpath to cross a field diagonally to reach a lane opposite Raikes Farm. Go right down the lane to find the Volunteer Inn at the bottom.

6 Retrace your step for 75yd from the inn and take the bridleway to the left. This leads past the gate to The Shieling and back to the double-trunked oak seen earlier.

7 After 130yd, keep to the left of the hedgerow and follow the public footpath and the poles over the crest and diagonally down across two fields and a stile, all the while admiring the views of the North Downs to your right. At the edge of a Woodland Trust copse, cross a stile and continue to reach a road. Cross the road and continue up the track opposite to reach a field and go across it.

8 At the trees turn right to exit through a gap lower down. Follow the track downhill for 80yd.

9 Then turn left through a gap in the trees. Cross the grassland to join a well made track for 330yd. Leave the track at the bend just past the bungalow, Twiga Lodge, and take the second, narrower path marked National Cycle Network route 22 and public bridleway.

10 Follow it to reach a road.

11 Turn right through a railway arch, keeping on the road to reach Gomshall Mill. There, cross the Tillingbourne and turn right, pass Tillings Teashop and return to the station by way of the approach road.

Norbury Park

Start At TQ158524, Crabtree Lane car park, RH5 6BQ

Distance 4¾ miles (7.75km)

Summary Moderate walking

Parking In the car park at the start

Maps OS Sheets Landranger 187; Explorer 146

Where to eat and drink The Stepping Stones, www.steppingstonesdorking.com. Open daily 11:00–23:00; Sunday 11:30–22:00

An interesting walk around Norbury Park, including a ruined chapel.

1 Turn right out of the car park, and after a few yards cross a stile into the field on the left. Go diagonally down the field to reach a stile halfway along the bottom boundary. Go over and drop down, passing through a gate and continuing through a field to a road.

2 At the road, turn left to reach a ruined chapel and the entrance to Chapel Farm. Continue along the road.

3 At the crossroads, follow Adlers Lane to the electricity enclosure by Treetops on the right.

4 Turn left here along the single-file path. Follow the path to the road.

5 Turn right (look out for the metal arrow in the road!).

6 At the railway bridge, turn left down a path to a field. Stay beside the railway and cross the River Mole.

7 Pass through a gate and make for the house to join a track.

8 After about 150yd along the track, turn left towards Lodge Farm on a roadway that bends across the river.

9 Just before the entrance to Lodge Farm, fork left then follow the path

around to the right keeping the house on your right. Go through a gate giving access to Swanworth Picnic Site.

⑩ Beyond the site join a bridleway heading right, which climbs gently under the trees.

⑪ At the junction at the top of the hill, turn right, past a wooden barrier and go down the snaking roadway, to reach the junction at the bottom. Turn left to pass Mickleham Priory and the farm buildings.

⑫ Fork left along the raised track to reach a cottage in a wood, and take the gated track going uphill.

⑬ The track rises steadily, passing under the railway and going over at a crossing to rejoin the road.

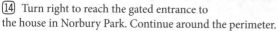

⑭ Turn right to reach the gated entrance to the house in Norbury Park. Continue around the perimeter.

⑮ Turn left at the picnic area, keeping the sawmill on your right and continue along the bridleway.

⑯ After just over ½ mile, fork right up the hill taking the bridleway and cycle route ahead, descending into the car park and the start of the walk.

Points of interest

Norbury Park – This area is a mix of wooded and agricultural land associated with its Georgian manor. In 2003 a small Bronze Age hoard consisting of two palstave axes and a scabbard chape dating from around 1150–1000 BC was discovered in woodland on the western side of the park. The park also contains an important grove of yew trees used by Druids for rituals and ceremony. They are some of the oldest trees of Great Britain.

Normandy and Ash

Start At SU926516, the car park on the A323, GU3 2DB

Distance 4¾ miles (7.75km)

Summary Moderate walking through fields, lanes and heathland

Parking In the car park at the start

Maps OS Sheets Landranger 186; Explorer 145

Where to eat and drink There are no refreshments stops en route

A varied walk from Normandy to Ash and back again.

① Turn right out of the car park and walk along the road to reach the garage, turn left immediately beyond it going over a stile. Cross the grassland, exiting to the left of a house to reach a road. Turn right to reach the front of the house, then take the footpath opposite.

② Beyond the gardens, keep ahead alongside a field and then veer half-left into the trees at the corner.

③ Cross a plank bridge and bear right, follow the fencing all the way around to the far corner and then turn right through a gate into a field.

④ Keeping the trees to your left, go forward in the direction of the metal mast. At an embankment, turn right and after 50yd take a track on the left.

⑤ Walk past the metal mast and to a T-junction. Turn left, then right to pass a house called Folly Hatch Farm.

⑥ At the road beyond, turn left up a rise. Keep right at the junction with Pound Farm Lane, and at the bend by another metal mast, you will reach the railway.

⑦ Do not cross the bridge into Ash Green Road but continue ahead to reach houses at the top of another rise.

⑧ Turn left past Pine Cottages and head for the spire of St Peter's church, Ash.

The path reaches the main road by the level crossing at Ash Station. Turn right and walk to a mini-roundabout. There, bear left up Ash Hill Road.

⑨ At the first turning on the right, Fox Hills Lane, take the wooded path by the road name sign and directly behind the 'Danger MOD Training Area' sign.

⑩ At the top of the hill and at a small clearing, turn right, to pass a pole. You will soon reach a diagonal crossing track.

⑪ Go half-left rising into the woods on an old concrete slab path to meet a track. Now keep ahead, passing through a clearing surrounded by conifers. At the junction, go ahead to a pole barrier.

⑫ Turn right following the fencing on your left, on a

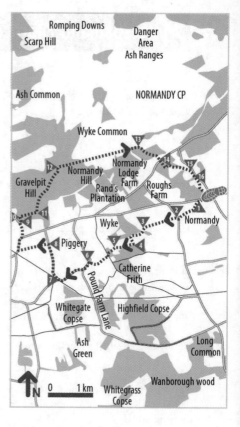

straight path which at two points crosses trenches. At the flag-pole beyond the last crest, you will meet a crossing rack, barred to the left.

⑬ Turn right here to reach a road at the rear of some houses. Go left to reach the road beside Hillside.

⑭ Cross and go down the stepped path to reach a sports ground. Bear left, keeping the grounds on your right and continue through the woods.

⑮ At the pavilion, go clockwise around a quarter of the field and then take the path leading to the recreation area. The car park and the start of the walk is a short distance beyond.

Wintershall and Thorncombe Steet

START At SU999398, Hascombe village fountain, GU8 4JG

DISTANCE 4¾ miles (7.75km)

SUMMARY A hard walk across fields and along trails and roads

PARKING On the road at the start

MAPS Landranger 186; Explorer 133, 134 and 145

WHERE TO EAT AND DRINK The White Horse, Hascombe, www. whitehorsepub.net

Enjoy wonderful geographical features and take a stroll through an open-air theatre.

1 Take the footpath opposite the fountain and cross the stream. Shortly after, turn right, heading for the houses. Upon reaching them, turn left to join the Greensand Way. Initially the walk rises steeply to join a track coming in from the right. After the barn, the track levels out.

2 Then turn left at a junction onto a narrower sandy path and following the Way.

3 Turn right at the T-junction, dropping down in a gully, and bearing left to reach a road. Turn right alongside the wall of Scotsland Farm, but only for 50yd.

4 Go left up the bank and follow the path through a wood and then across an open meadow. This is the site of the Wintershall open-air theatre.

5 Pass through the gate to join a stony track and on the bend bear left up the steep grassy hillside.

6 Cross the track at the top. The path descends diagonally to the bottom right corner. Over to the left there is a house with distinctive blue window frames.

7 Go left along the drive. Beyond the barn, keep to the field perimeter beside the wood to reach Gatestreet Farm.

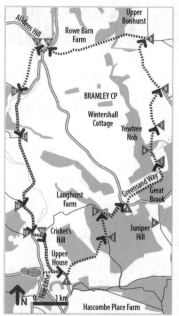

⑧ Turn left to pass Keepers, and maintain direction to reach an offset four-way junction.

⑨ Here, leave the Way and turn left into a field, climbing straight up the centre. At the top, cross a stile and go up two steps. Bear left and go through the woods to reach another stile. Keep ahead then descend keeping to the right side of the grassy bowl to reach a stile just below a telegraph pole. Go over and continue down to reach a road.

⑩ Turn left along Thorncombe Street. At the junction, turn right.

⑪ Then go left just beyond the stream. Follow the path left and proceed through a couple of fields to reach the drive of Phillimore Cottage.

⑫ Drop down to the road and turn right. Walk past four prettily painted houses and keep going to reach the lower car park of the National Trust-owned Winkworth Arboretum.

⑬ Enter if you wish to explore further or carry on up the road.

⑭ Turn left at the junction by Winkworth Farm onto the main road and with great care, crossing on the bends where necessary, continue for 400yd to reach Pine Cottage and Yew Tree Cottage.

⑮ Turn left onto a bridleway.

⑯ At the T-junction, turn right. Keep ahead at the Mill Lane turning and then turn right 200yd further on to get back to the start.

Points of interest

Wintershall – A privately owned house that puts on biblical productions.

Alfold and the Wey and Arun Canal

START AAt TQ027351, Sidney Wood car park, off Dunsfold Road, GU6 8HU

PARKING Car park at the start.
Maps: OS Sheets Landranger 186; Explorer 134

DISTANCE 5 miles (8km)

WHERE TO EAT AND DRINK Nothing en route

SUMMARY An easy and level walk through forests and fields

A peaceful walk along a disused stretch of canal and the surrounding countryside of Alfold.

1 Leave the rear of the car park by the information board and go to the right of the 'Dogs strictly under control please' sign. Meander through the woods on the main path, bearing slightly right and ignoring all public footpath signs. Pass a barrier to emerge onto a forest road. Turn right.

2 At the crossing at the corner of the Sedgehurst paddock, go ahead into the trees. The path curves left and after roughly 400yd you reach a memorial seat. Less than 100yd beyond, look for the bed of the old canal on the right.

3 Climb onto the raised embankment running along the other side. Stay on the embankment to reach a track, set back from which is a large white house.

4 Turn left, through a barrier and re-enter Sydney Wood. At another barrier and a lodge, turn right for a few yards.

5 Then go left along a bridleway to rejoin the canal. Keep ahead for just over ¾ mile.

6 At the junction of Gennets Bridge lock and the Sussex Border Path, turn left onto the bridleway to Oakhurst Farm. Walk along the drive.

7 Leave the drive just around the first bend, going left onto a footpath. Cross three fields to a belt of trees.

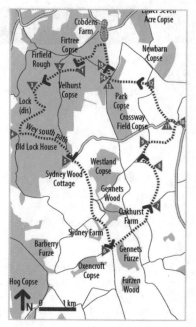

8 At the wooden kissing gate, turn left skirting Turtles Farm. Cross a stile, turn right, then pass through a metal gate. Continue alongside a horse track looking for a stile on your right.

9 Cross and take the stile opposite heading for Alfold church, crossing paddocks and more stiles.

10 At the end of the cemetery driveway, turn left and go along the lane.

11 Just past Bucklands, take the path on the right. Cross two fields to a farm drive and continue across towards the red building.

12 About halfway through this field, turn left through a kissing gate. Cross the field, two more gates and aim for the wood ahead. Enter and go forward for 180yd to reach a crossing.

13 Turn right for 10yd, then left and right once again behind the 'Riding by permit only' sign. Keep ahead to reach a stile.

14 Do not cross, but take the woodland path parallel to the field. Continue for the length of the field, and shortly after, bear left to return to the car park.

Points of interest

The Wey and Arun canal – The canal was constructed during the Napoleonic Wars, between 1813 and 1816 for the purpose of carrying coal, chalk and farm produce. It closed in 1871. However, in 1970, the Wey and Arun Canal Trust was set up to restore sections of the route. When restored, it will be an inland waterway link from London, via the rivers Wey and Arun, to Littlehampton on the Sussex coast.

Ashtead Common

Start At TQ179633, Chessington South Station, KT9 2JR

Parking Limited on-street parking at the start

Distance 5 miles (8km) or 7¼ miles (11.5km)

Maps OS Sheets Landranger 187; Explorer 146 & 161

Summary Easy level walking through fields and woodland

Where to eat and drink None en route

Tranquil areas are enjoyed on this walk close to one of the country's biggest theme parks!

1 From the station, turn right to reach the A243. Cross and walk along the lane to the entrance to Winey Hill opposite Virginia Cottage. Take the path through the gate and ascend to open grassland. Aim for the distant fenced pond, then continue ahead dropping down and through a gate skirting Chessington World of Adventures.

2 At the Leatherhead Road stile and signpost just before the wood, turn left and descend to the road. Cross and continue along the path opposite to reach another road.

3 Cross and walk diagonally across the grassland, heading for a wood and a white coal tax post.

4 For the shorter walk, turn left along the fringe of the woodland to reach the next coal tax post.

For the longer walk, continue ahead into the wood. Soon, bear right following Bridleway 33. After roughly ¾ mile a concrete bridge is reached.

5 Turn left and walk parallel with houses. At the end of the houses, keep ahead bearing left to face a metal gate to private woodland. Turn right in front of this and continue through the wood to a junction with a notice board.

6 Turn left and after 300yd pass a house and a few yards later a pond

and a bench. Keep straight ahead. At the Woodcock post, there is another coal tax post to the left. This is where the two walks join.

⑦ Turn right to reach Stew Pond. Walk around this to reach some steps leading to the Great Pond. Explore further if you wish, then return to Stew Pond to complete its circuit. Turn right to rejoin the earlier path marked Winter Horseride. After 350yd, the path reaches a road (the B280).

⑧ Cross and follow the Horton Lane sign to reach West Park Hospital and the Noble Park estate.

⑨ Take the footpath to the right of the entrance to Noble Park and after around ½ mile cross a stile into a field. Walk to reach a road at the bottom and go on to meet another by the gate to Park Farm. Turn left for 250yd.

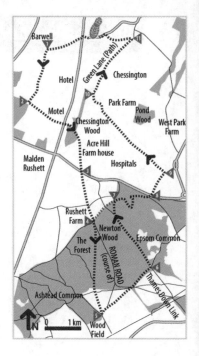

⑩ Pass Monks Cottage and go right along a path to join a road. Keep ahead to the end of a golf course.

⑪ Turn left at a signpost opposite Twin Elms to reach another road. Turn left to return to the station.

Points of interest

Great and Stew Ponds – The Great Pond is a wildlife reserve for pondlife, amphibians and resident wildfowl such as coots, moorhen, mallard, tufted duck, great crested grebes, swans and herons. The water is also visited by less common wildfowl in the winter. Stew Pond is the only pond in which fishing is allowed and is used by the CALPAC angling club.

Bletchingley and South Nutfield

Start At TQ327507, The Whyte Harte Hotel, Bletchingley, RH1 4PB

Distance 5 miles (8km)

Summary Moderate walking with plenty of stiles and mainly across mildly undulating fields

Parking On the road near the start

Maps OS Sheets Landranger 187; Explorer 146

Where to eat and drink The Whyte Harte Hotel, Bletchingley, www. whytehartehotelbletchingley.co.uk

The walk is bisected by the busy M23. Peaceful areas are enjoyed nearer to the two villages.

① Cross the main road to the Parish Church and go through the churchyard, keeping to the left. At the end of the surfaced footpath, continue to the junction facing some steps. Turn left. Cross the main road, continuing down Castle Square past the site of the village pound, last used in 1899.

② At the junction, take the far right public footpath rising above the private road. Along this stretch, enjoy the view of some fine houses and a lake.

③ At the bottom, and at a track coming from the gated field on your right, cross the stile and immediately cross the next on the right. Keep to the right of the field to go under the motorway (the M23). On exiting, take the path straight ahead to join a tarmac driveway leading to a road by Hawkesbury.

④ Turn left and walk to a bend. Drop down and cross the stile.

⑤ Keep to the left side of the field and go through a metal kissing gate. Continue ahead, keeping to the left of the dividing fence, and aiming for the next metal kissing gate.

⑥ Now walk into South Nutfield. Turn left along the street, pass the Village Hall and as far as number 124.

7 Turn left onto a gravel driveway with a fingerpost and follow it to its end. Bear half-right just beyond the Scout Hut. Cross two fields and then carefully cross over the railway tracks.

8 Bear left and take the cindered track, keeping the woods to your right and a field to your left. Continue along the surfaced path to reach a road. Turn left for 30yd.

9 Then walk up the drive signposted to Kings Lodge. Turn left beyond it to cross the M23. Follow the path to reach a road.

10 Then take the bridleway past the converted barn of Henhaw Farm.

11 After 50yd, opposite Cherry Tree Cottage, turn left and cross two fields to reach the railway again. Use the metal steps to go up and with great care, cross the tracks. Walk ahead for ¾ mile, and through several fields, to pass a barn.

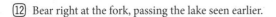

12 Bear right at the fork, passing the lake seen earlier.

13 At Castle Hill Farmhouse, go up the drive to meet the previously visited junction. Turn right. The path leads to a road. Turn left to return to the start.

Points of interest

Kings Lodge – The Kings Lodge Centre for Complex Needs cares for adults with brain injury and long-term neuro-degenerative conditions. In 2014 a £3m extension of the brain injury centre was completed.

The Devil's Jumps and Frensham Ponds

START At SU858418, Frensham Little Pond car park, GU10 3BT

DISTANCE 5 miles (8km)

SUMMARY A hard walk with two very steep climbs

PARKING In the car park at the start

MAPS OS Sheets Landranger 186; Explorer 145 and 133

WHERE TO EAT AND DRINK The Tern Cafe, Frensham Little Pond, www. nationaltrust.org.uk/frensham-little-pond

Bel & The Dragon, Churt, www. belandthedragon-churt.co.uk

A varied walk including an ascent of one of the Devil's Jumps and a walk around Frensham Little Pond.

1 From the car park, walk around Frensham Little Pond in a clockwise direction. After ½ mile, the path leaves the waterside and reaches a conifer-lined fence on the left. Continue straight on this path to reach the far end through a pole and concrete barrier.

2 At the junction, take the turning to the right, which goes alongside a garden fence, to reach a road. Turn right along the road for a few yards, then go left through a metal gate by a stone wall.

3 Enter the forestry and continue ahead, away from the road.

4 After 200yd turn sharp left. Follow the fence line for ¼ mile until you reach a pond on your right and continue ahead to cross a plank bridge.

5 Then turn right onto a sandy bridleway just beyond a footpath. Keep ahead on the bridleway towards the Devil's Jumps.

6 In around ¼ mile, begin the ascent of the hill at the end of the sandy track. There is a fine all-round view from the top, with the lake you walked past clearly visible. From here it is possible to turn left just before the rocky summit and swing right descending to reach a road and the Bel & The Dragon pub.

7 To continue from the summit, look south-west, facing the other Jumps, and take the narrow path down.

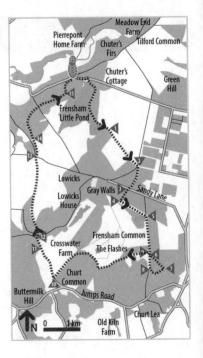

8 Turn right onto a track at the bottom.

9 At a junction, turn left and follow the wooden boundary fence past the grassy slope of the middle Jump, and continue along the bridleway for almost a mile to reach a road with signposts for Tanglewood and The Point.

10 Turn right, passing a nursery.

11 Shortly after, join a sandy ascending path.

12 Take the bridleway in front, but to the right, which over the course of around ½ mile, climbs to the various benches and viewpoints. Frensham Great Pond will come into view on the left, followed by a resighting of the Little Pond to the right.

13 At a junction, carry on ahead on the smaller right-hand and initially parallel track. It will soon start to descend.

14 Just after entering woodland, veer slightly right and beyond a crossing track, go uphill to find the Little Pond below on your right.

15 Turn left to descend steeply and return to the car park.

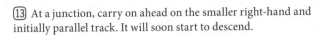

Points of interest

The Devil's Jumps – These are sudden hills, or knolls, and form part of a fragmented line of sandstone that stretches to Folkestone in Kent.

Farthingdown and Happy Valley

START At TQ308557, Chaldon church, CR3 5AF

MAPS OS Sheets Landranger 187; Explorer 146

DISTANCE 5 miles (8km)

WHERE TO EAT AND DRINK Nothing en route, but Fanny's Farm Shop in Merstham is worth a visit, www.fannysfarm.com

SUMMARY An easy level walk through woodland and along wide grassland

PARKING Available at the church

Enjoy the surroundings of a peaceful valley and some fine views from a ridge.

1️⃣ Walk down to the left of the triangle and turn left along the road for 50yd. Turn off right into a field and proceed over the crest to enter woodland on the far side. Descend for a few yards to reach a plank seat and finger post, signposted for the 'Downlands Circular Walk' and positioned at the top of a wide valley.

2️⃣ Turn left and keep at the same level for a little under ½ mile to reach Devilsden Wood.

3️⃣ Keep ahead as it rises to the open ridge of Farthingdown, by some buildings.

4️⃣ Cross the road and walk along the wide grassland. At a pair of spreading trees, pass an ornate finger post with directions to Hooley, Coulsdon, Purley and Chaldon. Keep ahead here, going gently down to reach the residential Downs Road.

5️⃣ Cross to the right side below the cattle grid, and return up the hill, taking the horse-ride, with the hedgerow to your immediate left. After just over ½ mile, look out for a fingerpost in the hedgerow at the beginning of a line of electricity poles.

6️⃣ Turn left here and drop down to reach Chaldon Way. Turn right along the road and where it ends, go forward along a path.

7 The walk is now taking you through Happy Valley. Keep to the valley floor all the way to the end to meet a track.

8 Turn right on this towards Leazes Avenue. Walk past several houses.

9 Just before a road, turn right onto the Tandridge Border Path. Follow the side of a field to a road. Turn right here to return to the start.

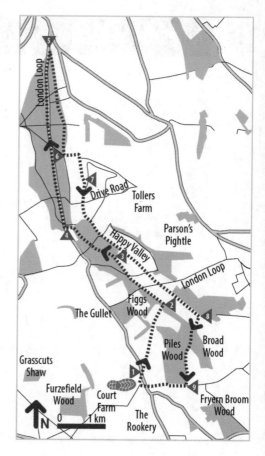

Points of interest

Farthingdown – Farthing Downs and Happy Valley is a Site of Special Scientific Interest (SSSI) for having the most extensive area of semi-natural downland habitats remaining in Greater London. Archaeological finds date from the Neolithic, Iron Age and Roman periods.

Kingston and Hampton Court

Start At TQ178693, south side of Kingston Bridge, KT1 1QN

Maps OS Sheets Landranger 176; Explorer 161

Distance 5 miles (8km)

Summary Easy walking on well-made deer park and riverside paths

Parking Available in numerous car parks in Kingston town centre

Where to eat and drink There are plenty of eating and refreshment opportunities in Kingston. The riverside restaurants are particularly pleasing

The magnificent Hampton Court Palace is the real feature of this walk. The grounds are free and it's time well spent admiring the topiary and grand planting schemes.

1. Cross Kingston Bridge and enter Hampton Wick. Follow the A308 left at the roundabout, passing the war memorial. At The Old King's Head, enter Hampton Court Park through the gates and follow the drive beyond the cattle grid.

2. Bear right at the first fork signposted 'Golf Club, Farm Cottages and Stud Nursery'.

3. Bear left at the second signposted 'Golf Club and Farm Cottages'.

4. At the end of the avenue of lime trees, the Palace is glimpsed above the embankment; head towards it on the far side of the Long Water. About halfway along, go left to have a look at the Medieval Oak, believed to be over 1,000 years old, then continue up to the railings guarding the Palace grounds.

5. Turn left to enter through the gate and spend time enjoying the lawns, flowerbeds, trees and shrubs.

6. When you are ready to return to Kingston, go around to the front

of the building and walk through the gate to reach the riverbank.

7 Turn left and walk along the pedestrian footpath with plenty of seats on which to relax and watch the river activity. Follow the bank all the way back to Kingston Bridge and the start of the walk.

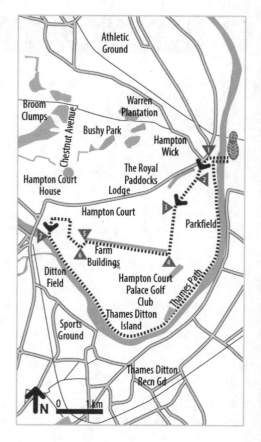

Points of interest

Hampton Court Palace – The Palace is a 15th Century Medieval Castle, standing in 60 acres of gardens which include the famous maze and house the annual flower show. It was originally built for Cardinal Thomas Wolsey, a favourite of King Henry VIII, around 1514.

Friday Street and Leith Hill

START At TQ128456, the Stephan
Langton, Friday Street RH5 6JR

DISTANCE 5¼ miles (8.5km)

SUMMARY Hard walking on uneven
and sometimes steep trails

PARKING Plenty of free parking is
available at the car park in Friday
Street 400yd from the start of the
walk

MAPS OS Sheets Landranger 187;
Explorer 146

WHERE TO EAT AND DRINK Stephan
Langton, www.stephanlangtonpub.
co.uk. Open for food Tuesday to
Saturday 12:00–14:30, 18:30–21:30;
Sunday 12:00–16:00. Closed
Mondays for food but open at 17:30
for drinks

Leith Hill Tower servery, www.
nationaltrust.org.uk/leith-hill/
eating-and-shopping. Open daily
from 1:000–15:00

A challenging walk in the heart of some beautiful countryside.

1 Go past the Stephan Langton pub on your left and walk up the
lane passing Lane End on your right. Go through a barrier and into
woodland. After just under ½ mile, you will reach a road. Go left and then
bear right onto a bridleway by the letter box set in the wall outside the
delightful Green Pastures. A further ascent follows through more pleasant
woodland. At a fork by a telephone pole, bear right, crossing a drive, and
continue to a road and turn left.

2 When you reach a junction, take the road signposted towards
Ockley. Turn off the road when you reach a track leading to High Ashes
Farm. Keep ahead ignoring the right turn to the farm itself, and also two
subsequent side paths, one on the right and one on the left.

3 At the T-junction facing a wooden gate, turn left to reach a road by a
car parking area.

4 Go across the road and follow the walker fingerpost for ¾ mile to
reach the tower on the top of Leith Hill. Continue the walk by taking the

steep path down the other side from the tower, going in the direction of the Landslip car park and Coldharbour Common, to reach a five-way junction at the entrance to The Dukes Warren.

5 Turn left down a gated bridleway and continue for about a mile.

6 Pass Warren Farm on your right and after just over another ½ mile you will reach a road with the Sariah Arabian Homestead opposite.

7 Turn right and immediately follow a footpath down a lane through the private Wotton Estate. Cross a stream, the infant Tillingbourne just starting out on its journey to join the Wey at Shalford, and then walk past a waterfall and pool, regrettably not accessible. Carry on along the track to pass a house.

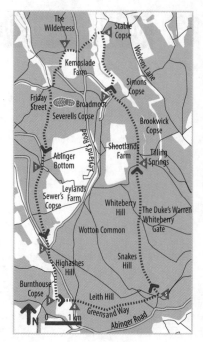

8 50yd past its entrance drive, go over a stile on the left. Cross the grassland beyond, and then climb steeply to reach a minor road. Cross and then keep ahead on the path beside a wood, into a dip.

9 Turn immediately left onto a narrow path. Now descend through the trees to reach the entrance to Kempslade Farm. Turn right along the drive and continue downhill at the road to return to the start in Friday Street.

Points of interest

Leith Hill Tower – Leith Hill is the highest point in southeast England at 965ft (294m). The tower was built by Richard Hull in 1766, and he is actually buried underneath it! On a sunny day, with a high tide, it is possible to see the English Channel through the Shoreham Gap.

Mickleham, Box Hill and Denbies Vineyard

Start At TQ170534, The Running Horses, Mickleham RH5 6DU

Distance 5¼ miles (8.5km)

Summary Hard walking using footpaths, steep steps and wooded trails

Parking On the road near the start

Maps OS Sheets Landranger 187; Explorer 146

Where to eat and drink National Trust café and servery, Box Hill, www.nationaltrust.org.uk/box-hill/eating-and-shopping

The Running Horses, Mickleham, www.therunninghorses.co.uk

A walk up to the most stunning viewpoint in Surrey, followed by a visit to Britain's largest vineyard.

① From The Running Horses, turn right and then turn left at the lych gate of St Michael's church, going along the drive to Eastfield Cottage. Beside the gates, cross a stile and follow a path uphill.

② After forking right, the gradient increases. Go ahead over a broad track, with the 'Mickleham Downs' sign to your left. Climb to the top of the ridge and descend slightly right. At the second iron stanchion, bear right to find a seat, from where you can look ahead to Leith Hill on the distant skyline.

③ Continue down the path, with the church spire of St Barnabas on Ranmore Common ahead. After 200yd, descend steeply via the steps.

④ Cross the road, pass through a car park and go up the track opposite. After 25yd, take the footpath on the left and go through a gate and climb to Juniper Top.

⑤ Enter the woodland along the lower path through a wooden gate and enjoy a level mile of walking. Continue past a compound on the left and at a T-junction shortly after, go right. Follow the narrow path ahead through the trees.

⑥ Just before the road, turn right to reach Donkey Green. If you wish you can stop for refreshment at the National Trust café.

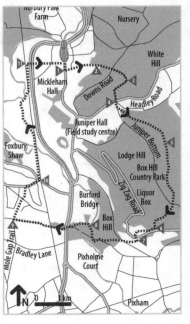

7 Locate the viewing platform and take the path in the direction of Hindhead. This is the North Downs Way, marked with the acorn logo of National Trails.

8 Just beyond the end of the grass slope, turn left at a post and descend via more steep steps to cross the River Mole by the stepping stones. There is a bridge downstream for when the water level is too high. Continue up to, and across, the A24, staying on the North Downs Way, which is just over to the left. Go through a railway arch and enter the Denbies Wine Estate.

9 After around ¼ mile there is a crossing. You can turn left through the vineyard to visit the Winery and Visitor Centre, or turn right to stay on the walk and head for Box Hill station, crossing one road and going right at the second, Chapel Lane.

10 At the railway bridge, turn left and go down a path to a field. At the far end of the field, cross the River Mole and, ignoring the path under the arch, make for a house. Join a track and, in 150yd, turn right to go under the railway to reach the main road.

11 Cross both carriageways and continue along Swanworth Lane to return to the start.

Points of interest

Denbies Wine Estate – The vineyards are situated on the North Downs with its famous chalky soil, in a protected valley of south facing slopes. The first vineyard was planted in 1986 and the wines now compete on an international level, winning gold awards in the sparkling, rose and dessert categories.

Peaslake and Holmbury St Mary

START At TQ086447, Peaslake
Village Stores GU5 9RL

DISTANCE 5¼ miles (8.5km)

SUMMARY A moderately difficult walk

PARKING Some parking is available
on the road or plenty is available
for free at the Hurtwood Control Car
Park 2, near the start of the walk

MAPS OS Sheets Landranger 187;
Explorer 145 and 146

WHERE TO EAT AND DRINK The
Hurtwood Inn, www.hurtwoodinn.
com. Drinks all day, food available
09:00–11:30, 12:00–14:30,
18:00–21:30

The Volunteer Inn, www.volunteer-
dorking.co.uk. Food served daily
from 12:00–14:30; Monday and
Tuesday 18:30 –21:00; Wednesday
to Friday 18:30–21:30; Saturday
12:00–21:00 and Sunday 12:00–
15:00

The Abinger Hatch, www.theabinger
hatch.com. Food served daily from
12:00–22:00; 12:00–21:00 on Sunday

Three villages are visited on this pretty walk through woodland.

1 From the cross, walk along Peaslake Lane, passing a car garage on your right, as far as the bend. Here, ascend a flight of steps and go left across the grass, passing the swings and continue on a path between fields to emerge at a lane. Turn left to reach a road and go a few yards up the drive past Barnfield and Timbers Ridge.

2 Turn right. Keep ahead, go over a stile, and cross an area of grassland. When you reach the trees, cross a stile and go down. Climb up the opposite bank and go over another stile to join a drive.

3 When the drive turns left by a telephone pole, go ahead up a path to reach a roadway. Turn left on this, going straight on down a hill between fields.

4 On a left bend, turn right at the barrier and follow the path to a road. Go left here then right onto a narrow descending footpath. At the bottom, go right onto the road to the Volunteer Inn in Sutton Abinger.

5 Continue up the road behind the inn, walking through a deep cutting.

6 After 100yd, climb the 37 steps on the right to reach a track leading away from the farm. Now as you walk towards the houses of Abinger Common, there are pleasant views of the North Downs to your left. Keep ahead to reach St James' church and walk through the lych gate.

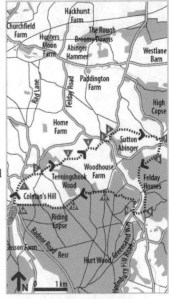

7 Cross the common outside the churchyard wall towards the playground. Go over the road and enter the field opposite by going up six steps and crossing the stile. Walk straight across to the woods and drop down to meet a path running under overhead wires.

8 Turn right to head in the direction of Holmbury St Mary. Walk past the first houses on your right and go through a gate. Continue ahead for ¼ mile until you reach a footpath on the right.

9 Take this path all the way to a driveway just after a brick wall and fenced section. Turn left to arrive at the village green. Turn right and follow the path around the bend. Cross the road to reach the telephone box.

10 Take the footpath on the right and climb steeply into woodland and then keep ahead on a broad path. Continue over a wide crossing track in a dip, to reach a car park on your right near the Youth Hostel.

11 Continue straight ahead and drop down to two ponds.

12 Go straight ahead and up to follow a sandy rocky path. Continue until you reach a meeting of several paths, keep ahead, bearing slightly right, to follow the yellow arrowhead.

13 Cross over the bridleway Riding Bottom and ascend to continue on the trail finally reaching a roadway by Tor Cottage.

14 Go down the steep bank opposite to return to the start.

Sutton Place and Holmbury Hill

START At TQ105459, The Volunteer, RH5 6PR

DISTANCE 5¼ miles (8.5km)

SUMMARY A moderate walk on quiet roads, wide sandy tracks and woodland trails

PARKING Limited road parking

MAPS OS Sheets Landranger 187; Explorer 145 and 146

WHERE TO EAT AND DRINK The Volunteer, Sutton Abinger, www.volunteer-dorking.co.uk

An opportunity to enjoy the vast area of The Hurtwood.

① From The Volunteer, turn right and walk up to the main road. Turn right again for 60yd to take the steps onto a narrow and steep footpath on the left.

② At the end of the footpath and opposite Stile Cottage, turn left and then immediately right through the pipe barrier and follow the fencing.

③ At the bottom, go through a wooden barrier and turn left.

④ Ignore a right turn and then take the footpath on the right. At the junction, go straight ahead following the road downwards. Cross the stile by the metal gate and go down some steps. Turn left at the end of the fence line to cross the bottom of a sloping field.

⑤ Pass through a gate and continue along the trail with woods to your right and gardens to your left. Cross the driveway and keep ahead to enter woodland.

⑥ At the 'Shere Parish Millennium Trail' post, turn sharp right and double back to go downhill to reach two ponds.

⑦ Pass between the ponds and turn left. Go forwards and upwards along the wide sandy firebreak for just over a mile to reach the Hurtwood Millennium Pinetum, marked with a plaque and cairn.

[8] Cross the broad track in front of you and continue along the well-made path passing a pond on your left and heading towards the open view. Continue along the path to the left, going through a 'Footpath Only' wooden barrier.

[9] Ascend through the trees and enjoy the view south on your right.

[10] At the top, pass through another wooden barrier and turn right to join the Greensand Way. Keep on this trail until the top of Holmbury Hill.

[11] When ready, and with the view behind you, go forward to the Hurtwood Control contribution pillar.

[12] Take the path to its immediate right. Keep ahead for just under ½ mile until a T-junction.

[13] Turn right and walk downhill for a further ¾ mile. As the track narrows, take the right fork to a trail that leads to a car parking area.

[14] Go through the car parking area passing the Holmbury St Mary Youth Hostel on your left. Carry along the Public Byway downhill as far as the 'Radnor Lane' road sign and the Woodhouse Farm barn.

[15] Turn up left into Woodhouse Lane and continue along the road until you reach a roundabout with a wooden bench.

[16] Turn left here to pass Little Thatch. Keep ahead on the road to rejoin the outward route of the walk. Turn right at Stile Cottage to take the narrow descending path to the main road. Turn right to retrace your steps to the start.

Ewell and Nonsuch Park

START At TQ226622, Ewell East
Station, KT17 1QL

DISTANCE 5½ miles (8.75km)

SUMMARY Easy suburban walking
with the addition of parkland and
riverbanks

PARKING On-street parking with
restrictions at the start

MAPS OS Sheets Landranger 187;
Explorer 161

WHERE TO EAT AND DRINK Nonsuch
Pantry Café, Nonsuch Park, www.
nonsuchmansion.com

An interesting and pleasant level walk with associations with Henry VIII.

1 Cross the road and turn into Nonsuch Court Avenue. Join Seymour
Avenue and at its end, enter a field. Follow the path towards a spire.

2 At 'Warren Farm' signpost, turn left. Head into trees and cross two
tracks to enter Nonsuch Park.

3 Turn right.

4 At a barrier, turn left along the Mansion drive. Pass the front, and
café, and follow the semi-circular path around the lawn to a hedge with a
paling fence and a black metal post.

5 Turn left and cross grassland towards a car park.

6 Here, turn left to pass obelisks. Beyond the third, bear right onto the
surfaced path and immediately left, heading for houses.

7 Just before the houses, turn right to walk parallel with them. When
the path disappears, go half-right to the remains of Nonsuch Palace's
Banqueting Hall.

8 Cross grass to the left of the remains and take steps down to cross the
A24.

⑨ Take the footpath to the left of the houses to reach a school.

⑩ Just beyond, enter the churchyard on the right. Pass the old tower to the new church of St Mary and leave by the lych gate. Go down Mill Lane 25yd to the right, entering the grounds of Upper Mill.

⑪ Cross the bridge and turn right. Follow the stream, crossing three more bridges. Go through a tunnel and turn right. Walk left along the riverbank to stepping stones.

⑫ Here, go half-right towards houses. Continue for 60yd.

⑬ If desired, enter Ewell Court Park at Gate 4 for a stroll around the lake. Then when ready, return to the gate and turn right. To continue without visiting the park, turn left at the gate and follow the surfaced path crossing the Hogsmill river. Keep left for 40yd then fork left.

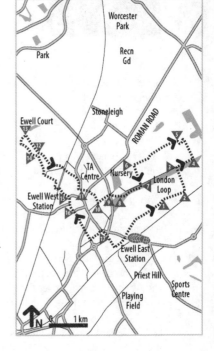

⑭ Emerge from trees, and follow the path around to the right to a residential road. Walk to a bridge and turn left up Eastcroft Road. Turn right at the top and left along an alley between Nos. 122 and 124. Cross the railway and follow the lane to a one-way system.

⑮ Turn right against the traffic then left, along the wall of Bourne Hall.

⑯ Go ahead into Lyncroft Gardens, along an alleyway. Cross the road, walk along a tree-lined avenue to Ewell High Street. Continue ahead along Reigate Road for 175yd, before turning left beyond No. 17. Follow the path to its end and turn right up Cheam Road to the A24. Cross on the right and take the track opposite.

⑰ Just before the bridge, turn left and return to the station.

START At TQ290533, Feathers Hotel, Merstham, RH1 3EA

PARKING On the bridge which crosses the M25 motorway.

DISTANCE 5½miles (9km)

MAPS OS Sheets Landranger 187; Explorer 146

SUMMARY Easy walking mostly through fields and woodland

WHERE TO EAT AND DRINK Fanny's Farm Shop, Merstham, www.fannysfarm. com

A surprisingly peaceful walk through this rural area mainly north of the M25.

1 From the Hotel, cross the main road into Quality Street and turn left at the entrance to the cricket club to join the North Downs Way. Follow the Way past the club, over the golf course and fields to a road. Turn right and enter the grounds of the Royal Alexander and Albert School.

2 Bear right at the first fork, skirting the school buildings, and continue along the drive to pass the Millennium Stones.

3 Leave the Way and ascend to reach Gatton Bottom. Cross and continue up the track opposite, passing under the M25. Follow the track past Crossways Farm to a junction with High Road.

4 Cross, and continue along Babylon Lane.

5 After 200yd, turn right through a gap in the hedge towards the brick house of Homefield Farm. Keep ahead, passing the converted barns, then go right through the gate with the convex mirror. Maintain direction to a junction.

6 Turn right onto the footpath. After 350yd turn right at the corner of a wood.

7 Now keep ahead, ignoring a left fork, until you reach a road by Keepers Cottage.

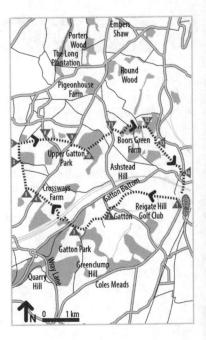

⑧ Cross the road and continue, going into and out of a dip and veering right across the grassland to reach a stile halfway along the far side.

⑨ Cross the stile onto a road. The entrance to Upper Gatton Park is to the right but the walk continues along the path beside Pilgrims. Continue on the grass, with the mansion visible to the right. Keep ahead to an area of woodland by the second of two bunkers.

⑩ Pass through the woodland, emerge and descend the left side of a sloping field, crossing into the adjacent field halfway down.

⑪ At the road at the foot of this field, turn left to reach a junction. At the junction, go right down Harps Oak Lane passing a farm and descending to Hoath Cottage.

⑫ Turn right at the yellow salt box and cross into the adjacent field beyond the swimming pool.

⑬ Walk diagonally across the field and aim for a point halfway along the top, cross the stile and maintain this direction to a residential road. Go right, downhill to reach St Katharine's Church.

⑭ After a visit to the church, follow the main road back to the start.

Points of interest

Royal Alexander and Albert School – Originally two schools, founded in 1758 and 1864 respectively, they merged in 1949. The school is one of only a tiny number of state schools in the country that is a true boarding school.

Pitch Hill and Holmbury Hill

START At TQ090409, The Bulls Head, Ewhurst GU6 7QD

DISTANCE 5½ miles (8.75km)

SUMMARY Hard walking due to some steep inclines and difficult terrain

PARKING On road parking available

MAPS OS Sheets Landranger 187; Explorer 145 and 146

WHERE TO EAT AND DRINK The Bulls Head, www.thebullsheadhotel.com. Breakfast served daily from 10:30; lunch 12:00–14:00; 18:00–21:00 and all day on Sundays and Bank Holiday Mondays

An energetic walk, but you are rewarded with fabulous views.

① From The Bull's Head cross the road and go down Wykehurst Lane until you reach a bridge with small brick parapets. About 25yd beyond, go right and climb up beside the edge of a field, passing through some woodland with a few steps, to reach a stile. Turn left here.

② Then turn right up the drive to reach Rapsley.

③ Go past the house on your right and continue straight ahead up the bridleway into the woods to reach a road.

④ Turn sharp right along the road, then go left into Moon Hall Road and uphill passing a letterbox.

⑤ After about 100yd go left at the public footpath sign and turn right shortly after to climb steeply straight up through the bracken and heather on a narrow path until you reach the very top of Pitch Hill with a triangulation pillar at the main viewpoint.

⑥ Take the sandy path behind the pillar going directly away from the view, and shortly fork right. Keep ahead past another vantage point, and continue for 400yd to reach a crossing. Turn right, then bear left continuing on the Greensand Way.

⑦ At a marker post, turn right. Follow the Way as it descends using steps and through a wooden gate to pass through the grounds of the Duke of Kent school and out onto a road.

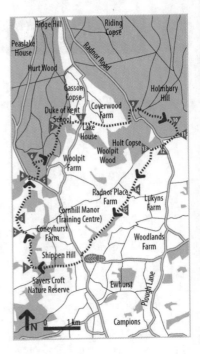

8 The path continues opposite and just to the left, crossing the valley. Follow the GW sign round to the left and then later to the right.

9 When a road is reached, cross and enter into The Hurtwood Car Park 1. Go through the car park and turn right between two concrete barrels following the GW sign. Drop down into a dip and go up the other side. Always following the GW signs, continue ahead and upwards taking a path that leads you up to the top of Holmbury Hill.

10 Facing the view, take the path to the left signposted 'the GW'. Shortly you will see a signpost: 'Bridleway 193 CAUTION Steep Slope Ahead'. Take this path!

11 At the bottom, turn right, pass the cottages and walk to the end of a brick wall on the left. Now take the path to be found immediately to the left of a white gate marked 'Wayfarers'. At the end of the path a wooden staircase leads down to a road. Cross slightly to the left, and then proceed down the drive to Radnor House.

12 At the low brick building, walk ahead on a concrete drive, then veer half-left by the pond beside a post marked 'Private'.

13 Just past the top of a rise, go left through a gate and cross a series of fields linked by stiles to reach a drive.

14 Cross the drive to continue on the clearly marked footpaths. Shortly, you will come to a concrete bridge used to cross a stream, after which you make for a gate in the woodland ahead.

15 Beyond this a crossing track is reached; keep ahead, following the yellow arrowheads to reach a road. Turn left here to return to the start.

Ranmore and Westcott

START At TQ146505, St Barnabas church, Ranmore RH5 6SP

DISTANCE 5½ miles (8.75km)

SUMMARY Hard walking

PARKING Limited parking is available opposite the church at the start

MAPS OS Sheets Landranger 187; Explorer 146

WHERE TO EAT AND DRINK Bertram Bees, www.bertrambees.co.uk. Open daily from 1:000–22:30; 1:000–midnight Thursday to Saturday and 1:000–17:00 Sunday. Closed on Monday

A varied walk. Stunning views make up for the extra effort required!

1️⃣ From St Barnabas church, walk along the road to the junction and the small group of houses, cross the grass to reach a gate by the red-brick cottages. The North Downs Way turns right at their rear but keep ahead making a steep descent following the 'Link to the Greensand Way' fingerpost. To the left you can see Dorking, straight ahead in the foreground is the village of Westcott and beyond you can spot Leith Hill Tower, the highest point in Surrey. Descend the grassy slope, pass through a gate to enter woodland and continue steeply down steps.

2️⃣ Cross the track and take more steps down to reach another gate which leads through a field to the railway line. Continue ahead crossing two fields, one with a gate, the other with a stile. At a third field, go alongside and at the end use the wooden railway sleeper bridge to join a farm track.

3️⃣ At the end of the farm track continue straight ahead through two metal kissing gates to reach the corner and some houses.

4️⃣ Turn left to join a bridleway.

5️⃣ At the start of the second field, go right and over a footbridge. Now follow the lane to the A25. Cross with care into Milton Street then keep an eye out on the right for a public footpath marker post on a grass verge.

6️⃣ Turn right here going over a wooden bridge. Whilst climbing, ignore the first alley to the right.

7 Take the second alley to the right, which runs between long walls of brick and stone. Follow it to the centre of the village. The walk continues by going left to pass a restaurant and then climbing up the hill leading to Holy Trinity church.

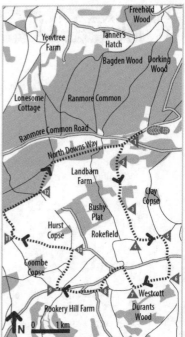

8 At the top of the hill take the path on the right. Go past the houses and go over a roadway to continue on the track which will return you to the A25 at the entrance to Rookery Drive. Go over the bridge.

9 Turn right into Balchins Lane and walk to the bend at the bottom.

10 Enter the field using the stile, and keep to the left. Go across four fields; the third and fourth are crossed diagonally to reach a small pond. Just past this, the walk reaches Coomb Farm.

11 Here, turn right and head for the hillside. The track leads you round to the right and after the railway bridge, you reach a gate; turn right and pass through to enter woodland. Just as you exit the woods, take the path half left to ascend steeply.

12 Keep left at the orange arrowhead. At the top you will join the North Downs Way. Turn right through a barrier and enjoy the views as you catch your breath. Continue ahead crossing the grassy expanse of Denbies Hillside and return to the start of the walk.

Points of interest

St Barnabas church – The church spire, nearly 150ft high, is a landmark for miles around and can be seen from other walks in this book. The church was built in 1859 to a design by the architect Sir George Gilbert Scott (1811–1878).

Shere and Albury Heath

START At TQ073480, Shere village car park, GU5 9HF

DISTANCE 5½ miles (8.75km)

SUMMARY A moderate walk on sandy and woodland trails

PARKING Free parking in the village car park

MAPS OS Sheets Landranger 187; Explorer 145

WHERE TO EAT AND DRINK Dabbling Duck, Shere, www.thedabblingduck. uk.com

The William Bray, Shere. www. thewilliambray.co.uk

William IV, Little London, www. williamivalbury.com

A most picturesque walk around the Shere and Albury Heath area.

① Exit the car park onto the road, turn left, then right up Middle Street passing the museum and pubs. Continue uphill away from the village and turn right into Pathfields. Beyond number 19, go ahead on a footpath rising into woodland.

② At a crossing, bear left and at the imminent fork bear right onto a footpath.

③ After 50yd, bear left onto a bridleway to reach a road. Cross the road onto the bridleway directly opposite leading you to a level crossing.

④ Go over, and turn right passing a line of cottages. After around ¼ mile you reach a footpath on the right at the corner of farm buildings.

⑤ Turn right and follow the path parallel with the driveway, cross the stile at the end. Follow the lane beyond almost to the railway bridge.

⑥ Turn left along Brook Lane to reach the junction with Brook Hill. Turn left for 80yd.

⑦ Then take the track on the right, passing Surrey Hacking Riding

Centre. Leave the track on the bend, and head for the wood on the skyline.

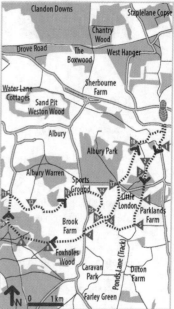

8 Inside the wood, follow the path through the break in the conifer plantation and keep ahead at the end, going over a crossing marked with a 235 post. Continue to enter a wide clearing, the hub of seven paths.

9 Exit by the broad track in the far right corner, descend to reach a lane by The Hame and some other cottages.

10 Continue to a bridge over a stream.

11 50yd further on turn right over a stile. Cross the pasture reaching fish breeding ponds and Ford Farm.

12 Take the drive beyond the gate, walking past the converted barns. At a T-junction, turn left and pass through the railway arch. Continue uphill and, near the top, notice a sandy area on the left.

13 Within 50yd fork right to reach Albury cricket pitch. Go forward to reach a road at the 'Woodside' post and continue opposite to an area of heathland. Cross the heathland to reach the cottages.

14 Turn right along the unmade Heath Lane. Pass Fircroft.

15 At a red brick out-building, turn left. At the cottage with a weather vane midway along its roof, fork left on a path to reach a road.

16 Turn left along Little London to the William IV pub, and continue on the track to the left of the road, up to South Lodge.

17 Take the footpath through the gate, following a line of trees.

18 At the foot of the slope is a cottage just above a ford and footbridge. Do not cross the stream, instead, take the path along the bank to return to Shere and the start of the walk.

Chelsham

START At TQ372590, The Coach House, Chelsham, CR6 9PB

DISTANCE 5¾ miles (9.25km)

SUMMARY Hard walking through valleys and fields

PARKING In the car park at the start

MAPS OS Sheets Landranger 187; Explorer 146

WHERE TO EAT AND DRINK The Coach House, Chelsham

Take on the undulating landscape to appreciate the terrific views of the London skyline on a clear day.

① Facing away from the chimneys of The Coach House, cross the grass, following the overhead lines, to the houses. Turn left and at the bungalow, turn right onto the footpath. Bear right reaching two metal gates at the end of the drive. Go through the left gate and keep beside the wood through a field. In the next, walk around the edge to the far right corner and cross a recessed stile.

② Keep ahead to enter another field.

③ Pass under the overhead lines and go through a gap in the hedgerow. Walk straight across the field to a pond by the exit to a road. Turn left and walk as far as Barnards Lodge.

④ Go through the white gate and up the drive for 100yd, turn right down a gravel path. The path descends quite steeply to a road.

⑤ Turn left to reach Warren Barn Farm after 400yd.

⑥ Turn left onto a bridleway, go through the farm and up a tree-lined track. Keep ahead ascending the valley and reaching the B269, Croydon Road.

⑦ Turn left, then, just over 100yd later, go right along the cart track.

⑧ Walk for ⅔ mile across the field and enter the wood through a gap in the trees.

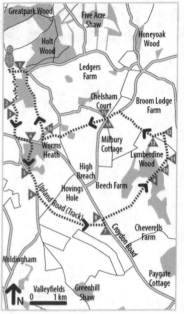

⑨ After 100yd, leave the main track and take the grassy footpath straight ahead. The grass path bears left, but you go ahead down a short, steep path, soon crossing a stile.

⑩ Descend half-left down the grassy slope reaching a gate at the bottom.

⑪ Go through and continue left, walking along the valley floor, going through another gate.

⑫ Follow the path around to the left to reach one more gate underneath overhead lines.

⑬ After 200yd, turn right to cross a stile and climb on a path inside woodland. Soon you will reach a road with terrific views of the London skyline. Turn left, passing Chelsham Heights.

⑭ Turn right into Washpond Lane. Enter the field opposite the fencing below the drive to Chelsham Court.

⑮ Walk diagonally across four fields to a crossing just beyond a stile. Here, go ahead to reach a minor road. Turn right for 80yd, enter a field to the left at a red and white barrier.

⑯ At the far end of the field, go through a metal gate to a road junction. Turn left to return to the start.

Points of interest

Chelsham – At an altitude of 250m, Chelsham has some commanding views over London and the South. It is one of the country's oldest villages, appearing in the Domesday Book as Celesham, where its assets were listed as: 1 church, 11 ploughs, from customary dues 1 hog. It rendered £15.

Chiddingfold

START At SU961354, St Mary's Church, Chiddingfold, GU8 4QA

DISTANCE 5¾ miles (9.25km)

SUMMARY Moderate walking through fields and some uneven woodland trails

PARKING On-street parking at the start

MAPS OS Sheets Landranger 186; Explorer 133

WHERE TO EAT AND DRINK Treacle's Tea Shop, Chiddingfold, www. chiddingfoldnews.org.uk/contacts/ the-green-room.htm

The Crown Inn, Chiddingfold, www. thecrownchiddingfold.com

The Swan Inn, Chiddingfold, www. theswaninnchiddingfold.com

A varied walk with modest ascents, and a visit to a donkey sanctuary!

① From the church, take the Grayswood road, keeping to the left of the pond. Just around the first bend, go up the footpath, climbing alongside the cemetery to join a residential road. When this turns right, keep ahead along an alley to reach an expanse of grassland.

② Walk along the top of this. After ½ mile, having crossed a drive and a paddock, you reach a road.

③ Turn right passing the entrance to Langhurst Manor. Go downhill to a road junction; turn right again.

④ After 200yd, just around a bend and just past Westerly, turn sharp left to reach the drive of Combe Court Farm. Keep right on the grassy footpath and cross two fields and three stiles to enter woodland.

⑤ Follow the path as it drops down to a stream crossed by way of a quaint brick bridge. Beyond, the path rises to a field leading to a railway line. Cross with great care. On the other side, beyond a field, more woodland is entered; bear right at a junction and follow a path down to a wooden bridge over a stream. Follow the track to pass the donkey sanctuary and to reach a road opposite a post box.

⑥ Turn right, passing the telephone box at the edge of Sandhills Common.

⑦ At a bend, follow the footpath sign. At the road crossing by Inglewood, turn right and cross the railway using the footbridge. On exiting the station, turn right to walk through the car park and yard.

⑧ Then turn left at the white gate to Lilac Cottage. Keep ahead on a grassy path between buildings. When a field is reached, go to the left of the tennis court and to a road.

⑨ Cross the road and take the footpath opposite. Beyond a wood, more grassland is reached. Walk diagonally towards a bridge. Cross and walk ahead to a broad grass track leading from a farm and turn left.

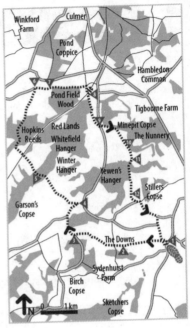

⑩ Just past the house, go up right and continue over the crest. Descend and aim for the metal gate.

⑪ Cross a stream and re-enter woodland. Climb gently, leaving the woods and passing through two fields to a line of bungalows.

⑫ Pass to the right of these and drop down to a road. Go left downhill and eventually turn right along Coxcombe Lane to return to the start.

Points of interest

Lockwood Centre for Horses & Donkeys – The centre's main business is rehabilitation and repatriation, but there is a herd of donkeys which can be spotted from the footpaths around the fields, with feeding times and grooming to be seen.

Beare Green and Leith Hill Tower

START At TQ176437, Beare Green pond, near Holmwood station, Beare Green RH5 4RB

DISTANCE 6 miles (9.5km)

SUMMARY Hard walking

PARKING Plenty of roadside parking

MAPS OS Sheets Landranger 187; Explorer 146

WHERE TO EAT AND DRINK The Plough Inn, www.ploughinn.com. Open daily from 12:00–23:00; Sunday til 22:30. Food served 12:00–15:00; 18:30–21:00

Leith Hill Tower servery, www.nationaltrust.org.uk/leith-hill/eating-and-shopping. Open daily from 10:00–15:00

A visit to both the highest pub and highest point in Surrey.

1. Walk up the road past the station, and take the footpath beyond the last house on the left. Continue to join a lane and proceed to Skinners Cottage.

2. Take the bridleway ahead, ascending to pass Moorhurst Manor. This becomes a stony path beyond a barrier of two tree trunks, rising to a fork between houses. Go right to join a road.

3. Follow the road around a bend to reach Kitlands East Lodge, and roughly 200yd further on, look out for a footpath fingerpost on the left.

4. Cross the stile and the field to reach a track. Follow this, passing Kitlands Cottage, and walk alongside the wall. Just past the entrance to Kitlands on the left, look out for a small grassy verge on the right.

5. Here, take the path leading you upwards and under overhead lines. Pass under a large oak tree to reach a metal gate. Go through and continue to reach a point just below Christ Church, Coldharbour.

6. Turn right on the road into the village to the Plough Inn.

7. Turn sharp left uphill and keep on the main track.

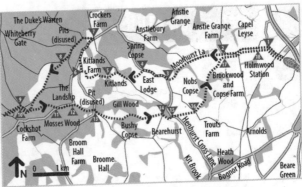

8 At the cricket pitch, take the byway to the left of the information board and keep on the main track for a little over ½ mile.

9 At a junction of paths, take the signed path to Leith Hill Tower. Once rested, retrace your steps back down the last hill.

10 At the junction of paths continue on an uphill track waymarked with an 'L-in-the-car' logo. Keep following the signs until you reach a road.

11 Go left along the road for 150yd to reach a bend.

12 Turn right onto a footpath and pass the memorial seat to Frank Longhurst. Continue downwards to reach another road. Cross, and walk for 50yd down a gravel drive.

13 Then turn left to cross the stile and go through a field, keeping initially to the left then heading for the top right corner to enter the next field. Go over a stile and head for the bottom right corner. Continue through the next field, keeping the trees close by on the right.

14 At the corner take the left path following the yellow arrowhead to reach a drive by a duck pond. Turn left to reach a road by Bearehurst Lodge and go across to reach the white gates of Trout Grange.

15 Follow the drive for 300yd and at the junction of paths keep ahead onto a track.

16 Stay on this track until it brings you to a road where you turn right.

17 Continue for ¼ mile before leaving the road and taking the footpath on the right.

18 Retrace your steps to the start.

Elstead and Tilford

START At SU908437, Elstead green, GU8 6HD

DISTANCE 6 miles (9.5km) or 8½ miles (13.5km)

SUMMARY The shorter walk is easy walking; the longer has a steep climb

PARKING Free street parking

MAPS OS Sheets Landranger 186; Explorer 145

WHERE TO EAT AND DRINK The Barley Mow Inn, www.thebarleymowtilford. com. Open: Summer 11:00–23:00; winter 11:00–15:00, 18:00–23:00

The Donkey, www.donkeytilford. co.uk. Open daily from 12:00

Both are charming woodland walks between pretty villages.

1 From the green, walk along Thursley Road to St James Church, and turn right into Westbrook Hill. Turn right along a bridleway.

2 After ¼ mile there is a junction; take the bridleway in the middle. Walk past Upper Hankley Cottage, signposted in a tree. Stay on the bridleway and after 100yd veer right. Keep right at the next fork. Pass a clearing on the left and drop down to Stockbridge Pond.

3 Continue along the track to reach the main road.

4 Turn right onto the track to reach the green at Tilford.

5 Turn right to cross the East Bridge.

6 For the shorter walk, continue up the road to reach a fork before a bend. Bear right along Whitmead Lane to reach the entrance to Whitmead 7a. Go along the byway for just under ¾ mile 8a. Shortly after passing Ravenswing, turn right along the byway to The Donkey pub. There, cross the main road and walk along the track opposite for 30 yards to rejoin the longer walk. The longer walk turns left opposite a telephone box, along a bridleway. Turn left along the drive passing an impressive house.

7 After 150yd, go right at a fork onto a byway to reach the road by

Sheephatch Farm. Cross and follow the byway to the foot of a gully.

⑧ Turn left along a sandy track to reach a road.

⑨ Turn right for 250yd to the end of the wall of Keeper Cottage Stud.

⑩ Go left along a bridleway passing Yew Tree Cottage, Crooksbury Cottage and the Waverley Cottages.

⑪ At a road, turn left for 200yd to reach Crooksbury Hill car park.

⑫ From the back of the car park, ascend Crooksbury Hill.

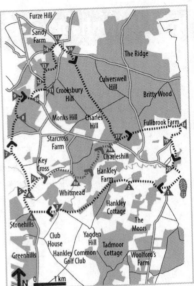

⑬ At the summit, turn right and, after a short descent, go left around a large house. At the barriers go left. At a small clearing with a junction of paths go straight ahead; the track now swings left. At another set of barriers take the more left path, while descending down to the road.

⑭ Turn right along Botany Hill into The Sands.

⑮ At the crossing, turn right towards Cutmill, passing another Barley Mow Inn. About 150yd beyond, turn right into Long Hill.

⑯ Follow the straight track for around 1¼ miles. Eventually you will come to some houses. Continue towards The Donkey pub.

⑰ Just 30yd before the road is reached, turn left up a bridleway to join a drive. Cross a road beyond the gatehouse to reach another path. At the end of this path, another road is reached, by the entrance to Fullbrook Farm.

⑱ Turn right and just past the entrance to Brookfield, take the footpath going left.

⑲ Keep on this path to the Wey, which is followed to a road.

⑳ Turn left over the bridge to reach Elstead and the start of the walk.

Puttenham and Cutt Mill

START At SU931478, The Good Intent, GU3 1AR

DISTANCE 6 miles (9.5km)

SUMMARY A moderate walk through undulating fields and along wooded trails

PARKING Road parking available at the start

MAPS OS Sheets Landranger 186; Explorer 145

WHERE TO EAT AND DRINK The Good Intent, Puttenham, www.thegoodintentpub.co.uk

A pretty walk just south of the Hog's Back and taking in part of the North Downs Way.

1. Walk along Suffield Lane, and then go ahead over a stile just past the gateway of Puttenham Priory. You have now joined The Fox Way. Keep ahead on this trail for a little over ¾ mile, going over stiles and passing through fields.

2. Join a road at a metal gate and continue ahead to reach a pond.

3. Turn right up the Public Byway to pass Lydling and continue along the byway, ascending and skirting an area of woodland on the right. The path now curls left under overhead lines.

4. When you reach a crossing about ¼ mile further on turn right and continue to the next marker post 350yd down the hill.

5. Turn right again to reach the drive to Rodsall Manor. Follow the drive left, going away from the house, to reach the end of the stone wall.

6. Just beyond, go ahead along a narrow bridleway and descend to Cutt Mill House. Walk along the drive to reach a lake.

7. Turn left up by the wooden posts to walk clockwise part of the way around the lake. Cross a stream, then a track, and go forwards along the bridleway to reach a road.

8 Turn right for 600yd to reach a crossroads.

9 Then turn right again and go over the causeway.

10 At the end of the causeway, turn left around the shoreline. The path veers away from the water to come to a junction.

11 Turn left and walk across a low bridge and up a rise. Keep ahead joining a broad track beside the fencing on your left. After roughly 300yd cross some planking.

12 Go past another pond on your right. The path now rises beside tall conifers. Keep on the bridleway until you emerge onto the openness of Puttenham Common.

13 Turn left and go ahead 100yd.

14 Turn right, keeping the fencing on your left as you start to descend.

15 Fork right shortly. Lower down, at the T-junction after a path has merged from the left, go left and take any of the paths ahead to reach the byway that is part of the North Downs Way.

16 Turn right onto the byway and carry on this path to return to Puttenham and the start of the walk.

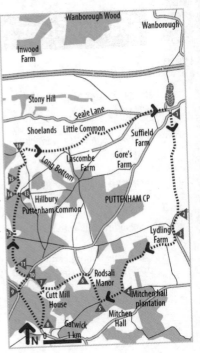

Points of interest

Puttenham Priory – The original house dates from 1266. In 1762, Thomas Parker built a handsome Palladian villa with gardens later designed by Gertrude Jekyll, and now fully restored. The Priory, which has an ice house, is now the home of Queen drummer, Roger Taylor.

Shamley Green

START At TQ052448, Hurtwood Car Park 8

PARKING Free car park at the start

DISTANCE 6 miles (9.5km) or 8 miles (13km)

MAPS OS Sheets Landranger 186 and 187; Explorer 145

SUMMARY A moderate track walk

WHERE TO EAT AND DRINK The Speckledy Hen, Shamley Green, www.thespeckledyhen.com

A secluded walk with lovely views and a Christmas tree farm!

1 Cross the road and take the bridleway into woodland. After ⅓ mile, turn left at a crossing to Mayor House. Walk up a rise to a left bend.

2 Turn right over a stile and climb up the right side of a field, going over a hill. Continue through several fields and over a Public Byway.

3 Keep ahead on the main track, pass a house, and a minor road signposted Keepers Cottage.

4 Cross the road and go straight ahead. Keep ahead at a path crossing to another road. Turn left, reaching the entrance to Hurtwood Car Park 5.

5 Turn in here and go through the car park. Take the steep path down to the right. Keep descending ignoring any crossing paths.

6 At the bottom turn right onto a bridleway which soon joins the drive from Alderbrook and leads to a road. Turn left here.

7 At the foot of the hill, turn right into Lapscombe Farm. Pass between the two houses and bear left to reach a lake. At the gate, go right. After 100yd a second lake comes into view.

8 Leave the track here, turning off left, crossing a stile. Go right, following the top side of a field. In the far corner, join a track and follow it into woodland, past a small pond. Walk uphill to a road opposite a gate and stile at the top. Turn towards a house and follow the boundary towards the lake. Head to the woods, joining the Greensand Way.

⑨ At a T-junction, turn right to reach a road and turn right.

⑩ Just beyond Stroud Farm turn left onto Greensand Way. Go across the foot of a sloping field to reach a drive leading away from Little Cucknells. Just past the gate, turn left. Continue past Reel Hall Cottages. At the road, turn left to reach Shamley Green.

⑪ Go up the narrow path to the left of the hedge beside the drive; the walks divide at the top by the house. For the shorter walk, turn right, and exit the field over a stile. Follow the fencing to the top of the rise ahead, and then bear right to join a track. Stay ahead on this for ¾ mile reaching a gate beside a road. Keep the gate on your right, and

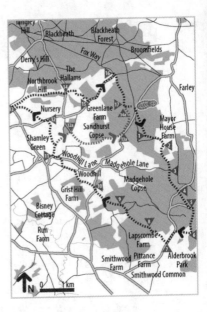

continue until you reach another gate on the left. Here, turn right and at the T-junction turn right again to return to the car park. For the longer walk, turn left and cross the fencing into the field on the right. Aim for the house ahead and join a track 100yd past it. Continue to reach a road.

⑫ Turn left to the entrance of Tree Tops. Take the path up the bank. After emerging into grassland, go half-right towards St John's Seminary. Cross three fields and pass a cottage. Follow the hedge to the road.

⑬ Turn right for 75yd then take the drive to Derryswood, on the right. Pass a cascade, and 100yd further on, go right through a gate. Go along a field and cross a stile just below a brick house.

⑭ Keep ahead to reach a road and go along the drive to Darbyn's Brook. At the end of the surfaced drive, go up a track to reach a road.

⑮ Turn left and go along for ½ mile to a grass triangle by a cottage.

⑯ Turn right, following a bridleway sign around the back of a garage. After 25yd, under the overhead lines, go right up a narrow path.

⑰ At the top of the trench section, turn left. Keep ahead and at the T-junction turn right to return to the car park.

Westcott to Friday Street

START At TQ142486, Westcott village green, RH4 3NR

DISTANCE 6 miles (9.5km)

SUMMARY Moderate walking along tracks and trails

PARKING On road parking dotted around the village

MAPS OS Sheets Landranger 187; Explorer 146

WHERE TO EAT AND DRINK Wotton Hatch, www.wottonhatch.co.uk. Open daily for drinks from 11:00–23:00; Sunday til 22:00. Food served daily 12:00–22:00; Sunday til 21:00

Stephan Langton, www.stephanlangtonpub.co.uk. Open for food Tuesday to Saturday 12:00–14:30, 18:30–21:30; Sunday 12:00–16:00. Closed Mondays for food but open at 17:30 for drinks

A very pleasant walk from a village to a pretty hamlet along leafy byways.

① From the green, walk down Westcott Street to the junction with Springfield Road, then take the path going left beside Fir Cones. The path skirts a lake and some back gardens before reaching the A25.

② Cross with care and go along Rookery Drive opposite, passing Mill House and two other delightful cottages with a stream flowing between them. Continue along the track, which veers left below a row of town-houses and then starts to ascend. At a fork, keep left and continue along the bridleway to reach a junction at the end of a cutting.

③ Take the second left following a sandy track for ½ mile.

④ At the end of the last field on the right, go right down into a dip and take the public footpath keeping the wooded slope on your left.

⑤ There is a stile at the bottom beyond which the route goes left for 100yd to reach a stile on the right, just past a gate.

⑥ Go over the stile and cross the grassland before climbing up a steep slope to reach a minor road. Cross and continue ahead on the path beside a wood, into a dip.

[7] Turn immediately left onto a narrow path. Now descend through the trees to reach the entrance to Kempslade Farm. Turn right along the drive and continue downhill on the road to reach Friday Street.

[8] Cross the bridge and turn right, continuing forward to pass a bridge on the left.

[9] Go over the stile by the gate. Keep ahead where a series of small lakes can be glimpsed through the holly bushes on your left. Follow the path and bears right.

[10] Shortly after bearing right, turn left. Descend using the wide steps to cross a meadow to join the drive of Wotton House.

[11] Turn right over the stile and continue 300yd along the drive.

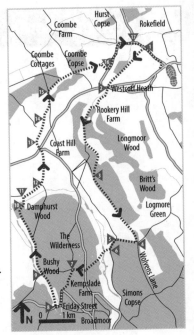

[12] Go over the stile on the right and cross the field diagonally in the direction of a village hall and the Wotton Hatch pub just beyond. Cross the main road and walk down the lane, towards the church of St John the Evangelist, for 100yd to reach a stile on the right.

[13] Go over the stile into a field and make your way down the little valley.

[14] Take the middle path between hedgerows, passing two small ponds on the right. When you emerge, keep straight ahead ignoring the path on the right and at the bottom cross another stile to reach a lane with a cluster of houses.

[15] Turn right along the track, which later becomes surfaced, to reach a T-junction.

[16] Turn left staying on the road.

[17] After crossing the bridge beyond the pink-painted Old Mill House, return up Westcott Street to the village green.

Newlands Corner and St Martha's

Start At TQ044493, Newlands Corner car park, GU4 8SE

Distance 6¼ miles (10km)

Summary A hard and lengthy walk with steep ascents and descents

Parking Plenty available at the start

Maps OS Sheets Landranger 186; Explorer 145

Where to eat and drink Tillings Cornerhouse, www.tillingscafe. co.uk. Open 08.30–16.30

The Percy Arms, www.thepercyarms. net. Open 11:30–23:00

Picture postcard views, industrial history and plenty of hills.

1 From the Visitor Centre, walk down the slope opposite to join a flint path veering right at the North Downs Way marker post. After about 20yd, immediately past the first trees, go left down the hillside. Cross a track and take the path through the copse ahead. Continue down the middle of a field to reach the building at the bottom.

2 Pass to the right of the house and, 100yd along the track, turn right to a road. Go across onto the bridleway to a car park. At the information board take the path to the left, following the green trail post.

3 At the junction with a four-way fingerpost, head down onto the footpath through holly bushes and trees. Now follows a picturesque stroll with the Tillingbourne at the base of the slope.

4 The path reaches a house; it is possible to circumnavigate the pond before continuing along the drive, going past another pond to reach a converted mill.

5 Cross a bridge over a sluice and turn right along a footpath beside a field. Now go over four stiles to reach a lane.

6 Cross the bridge ahead and immediately turn left along the bank going past a large pipe. You will soon pass the ruins of the gunpowder factory. After 200yd an area with picnic benches is reached.

⑦ You can turn left here for The Percy Arms opposite Chilworth station. This detour will add ½ mile to the walk. Otherwise continue along the path, passing a row of millstones. An information board about the Chilworth gunpowder factory is situated just before the road (Blackheath Lane).

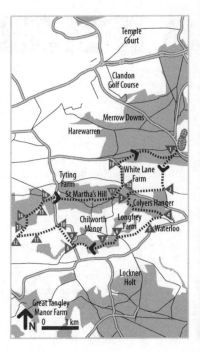

⑧ Turn right along the road and at the bend, go left.

⑨ At once fork right up a path.

⑩ At the top, turn left and enter the field by the post box. Walk along the field's lower side, passing a barn in the dip.

⑪ At the foot of the following rise, go right over a stile, up through the field beyond to reach another stile.

⑫ Go over the stile and climb to a hilltop for a fine view.

⑬ Go forward to reach the edge of the woods and turn right along a grassy path.

⑭ Walk past a camp site, then enter the woods descending to meet the road beyond the metal barriers. Turn left along the road for 20yd.

⑮ Follow the North Downs Way on the right to the top of St Martha's Hill. Then rejoin the North Downs Way, taking the sandy track downhill.

⑯ At the signpost with the acorn logo, bear left towards a road. Just before the road, turn left and then immediately right to continue on the North Downs Way running alongside White Lane and going past the farm.

⑰ A little way up the hill, cross the road, and return to Newlands Corner by walking across open downland.

The Downs Link Path and Wonersh

START At TQ031472, Chilworth Station, GU4 8QN

DISTANCE 6½ miles (10.5km)

SUMMARY A moderate walk along well made tracks and drives

PARKING On-street parking

MAPS OS Sheets Landranger 186; Explorer 145

WHERE TO EAT AND DRINK The Percy Arms, Chilworth, www.thepercyarms.net

The Grantley Arms, Wonersh, www.thegrantleyarms.webstarts.com

A walk along the path that links the North and South Downs.

1 From the station, go along the A248 towards Dorking for ¼ mile, passing a duck pond, and turn right by the bus shelter to join the Downs Link Path. This path is now followed as far as Bramley, navigation made easy by the fingerposts and logos. Beyond the railway bridge, go ahead, and in under ½ mile reach a drive.

2 Cross half-right and proceed through the woods. To the left of a clearing there is a memorial cross from where you have a clear view up to St Martha's church. The path turns left onto a track and crosses a road. The sign for Blackheath is just on the left.

3 Continue ahead and pass Great Tangley Manor. After about ¼ mile and shortly before the busy road, look out for a right turn.

4 Turn right here, continuing on the Downs Link to reach the road. Cross the road and then go anti-clockwise around the base of Chinthurst Hill before reaching a road close to Southlands.

5 Go ahead along Tannery Lane, and turn down left just before the bridge.

6 You will notice that a smaller bridge nestles beside the one carrying the road: go over this and down to the track of an old railway. Turn left to reach Bramley and Wonersh Station; the platform and nameboard

still remain, and an information board about the Downs Link Path is present.

(7) At the road beyond, leave the Downs Link Path and turn left. Cross the stream and follow the road to the right into Wonersh. At the Grantley Arms, keep ahead towards Shamley Green.

(8) Then go along Barnett Lane.

(9) A few yards past Woodyers Close, turn right on a gravel drive towards a metal gate and climb the path up Barnett Hill.

(10) At the top, walk past a house and about 100yd further on, fork right off the drive. Descend, then cross the gravelled entrance to the Wonersh and Blackheath cemetery.

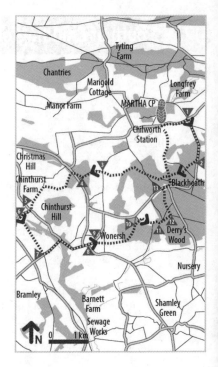

(11) At the junction by a blue marker post, climb steeply right to emerge at the top onto heathland.

(12) At the end of an enclosure of conifers, turn left. Keep ahead for just over ¼ mile to emerge beside St Martin's church in Blackheath village.

(13) Turn right to reach the crossroads, then go left along Sample Oak Lane for almost ¾ mile to return to the station.

Points of interest

The Downs Link – Following the route of two disused railway lines, it is a 37-mile (59km) footpath and bridleway linking the North Downs Way at nearby St Martha's Hill with the South Downs Way near Steyning in West Sussex.

South of Chiddingfold

Start At SU961354, St Mary's Church, Chiddingfold, GU8 4QA

Distance 6½ miles (10.5km) or 11½ miles (18.5km)

Summary Moderate walking on both of these walks

Parking On-street parking

Maps OS Sheets Landranger 186; Explorer 133

Where to eat and drink The Mulberry Inn, Chiddingfold, www. themulberryinn.co.uk

1 Walk down the road and cross a bridge. Past Turners Mead, turn left up a path. Beyond the gardens, cross a stile, go ahead, bear right and descend. Cross a stile into woodland, at the top turn right over another to a field.

2 Turn left and continue along the field boundary. Re-entering the wood in the corner, take steps down to a lake.

3 Follow the path to grassland and keep ahead, crossing a stile and continue down the drive of Old Pickhurst to a road.

4 Turn right. Beyond Corrie Mead, go left.

5 Half way through the field, cross a stile on the right. Cross another stile, then follow the overhead lines, keeping to the right, to go through a gate. Cross a field to a road and Robins Farm Racing Stables.

6 Go left past the entrance, taking the footpath on the right; keep right of a paddock. Keep ahead at the fingerpost and head for the fingerpost by the hedgerow. Turn right towards the overhead line pole by the wood.

7 Enter the wood via the plank bridge. At the top, cross a field and a stile. Follow around to the right and skirt Garden Cottage to a road. For the shorter walk 8a take the path opposite. Go through a gate and keep left across a field. Cross three more fields into a wood. After 60yd, turn right to reach a track serving Gostrode Farm. Turn left to reach the A283. The Mulberry Inn is on the left 9a .To continue, go 180yd right. Then turn left along Killinghurst Lane 10a . After ¾ mile, at a left bend, rejoin the longer walk.

⑧ For the longer walk, turn left and walk to a junction. Go left.

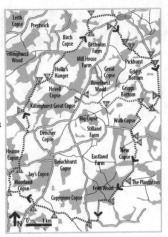

⑨ Then keep ahead at a bend over a cattle grid.

⑩ Go right at a fork below The Deer Tower. Keep left and descend to corner of field. Beyond gate cross bridge to skirt field and pass through a gap. Bear right uphill to a field with fingerpost.

⑪ Continue to a house and walk beside a wall.

⑫ After 500yd, at a left bend by a gate, turn right into woodland. After 50yd go half-left. Bear to reach Northchapel. Turn right to reach the main road. Turn left and cross.

⑬ Take the path beside Central House. Walk across fields.

⑭ Turn right at the footpath to Upper Diddlesfold Farm.

⑮ Keep by a barn, then go right into a field. Cross two stiles.

⑯ Ascend the bank up a field. At a gate, enter a field on the left and continue to a drive. Turn right and at the tennis court, cross a stile to a road.

⑰ Turn right to a junction, then descend by bearing right.

⑱ At the Old Hearne Farm entrance, take the path parallel with the drive, passing Anstead Brook Stud to the road. Take the path opposite, going around a field towards the house. There, go left to a road.

⑲ Walk right, pass parkland on the right, and reach a road junction.

⑳ Keep ahead and at the first bend, rejoin the shorter walk.

㉑ Go ahead and after ½ mile cross a stream. At the T-junction, turn right past Hollyhurst. At Sydenhurst House turn left along the drive. Go left of the garage and a lake. At the top, cross a stile. Aim half-right.

㉒ Beyond another stile, the path reaches a residential road. At the end of the road, descend to return to the start.

Haslemere and Blackdown

START At SU904328, Haslemere Town Hall in the High Street

DISTANCE 6¾miles (10.75km)

SUMMARY Hard, and at times, hilly walking

PARKING Public Car Parks in the town

MAPS OS Sheets Landranger 186; Explorer 133

WHERE TO EAT AND DRINK Nothing en route

1 From behind the Town Hall, ascend College Hill, beside Barclays Bank. At the top, turn left along Hill Road.

2 Turn right up Old Haslemere Road and at the T-junction, turn left along Scotland Lane for 150yd.

3 Just before Denbigh Road, turn right down between Littlecote and Oakhurst. At the bottom is Stedlands Farm.

4 Turn left, cross the stream and enter West Sussex. Follow the Sussex Border Path (SBP). Pass Valewood Farm House after 300yd.

5 Then, after about 100yd, turn left up the track.

6 Ignore the first gate but around the bend, take the gate right onto a bridleway to climb the hillside. Go right at the top.

7 At the end of the next field, go through a gate and turn left uphill.

8 At another gate and a post with several trail markings, fork right entering woodland.

9 At the next fork, before a gate, go up left. Bear right at the top and straight over at a crossing. Walk on the broad sandy path for under ½ mile, veering right at a junction.

10 At a fingerpost within a triangle of grass, go right leaving the SBP. Carry on the wide trail.

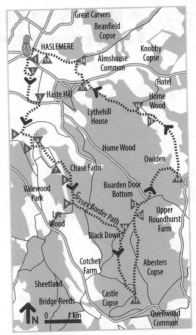

⑪ At the top of Blackdown, at 917ft, and at a fingerpost, go ahead for 100yd to drop to the viewpoint for south-east views. When ready, return to the fingerpost and go right on the wide track for roughly ¾ mile.

⑫ Rejoin the SBP and keep ahead.

⑬ Before the car park, near the NT donation pillar, follow the Serpent Trail taking the right bridleway down to a road. Walk downhill, leaving the SBP.

⑭ In under ½ mile, at Barfold, turn left passing three bollards. Continue for just over ½ mile to a dead-end.

⑮ Turn right through a gate passing High Barn Farm. Bear half-left down the field entering Barfold Copse.

⑯ Continue to reach the B2131. Cross, and turn left.

⑰ At the end of the grassy bank, take the footpath dropping down and eventually turning right alongside a fenced field. Pass through two gates and keep ahead to a junction where there is a NT sign for Witley Copse and Mariners Rewe on the right.

⑱ Turn left, cross the stream and walk through two fields to a drive. Continue ahead, passing NT barns on the left.

⑲ After 300yd, turn right through a gate and climb the slope. At the top, go up steps and through the car park to return to the High Street.

Points of interest

Blackdown – A favourite of Tennyson, the area is covered with heather and pine trees and has miles of secluded walks, sunken lanes and drove ways.

Wisley and Ockham Mill

START At TQ067610, The Blue
Anchor, Byfleet, KT14 7RL

DISTANCE 6¾ miles (10.75km)

SUMMARY Easy walking through
woods, fields and along the canal

PARKING On-street parking

MAPS OS Sheets Landranger 187;
Explorer 145 and 160

WHERE TO EAT AND DRINK The Blue
Anchor, Byfleet. www.the-blue-
anchor.co.uk

The Anchor, Pyrford Lock, www.
anchorpyrford.co.uk

A tranquil walk along the canal with a chance to visit RHS Wisley en route.

1 From the pub, cross the road into Church Lane and walk by the wall of Clock House, passing four bollards. At the end, turn left into Mill Lane and pass the garden centre, eventually reaching the River Wey.

2 Turn right onto the bridleway by the bridge to 'Bluegates Hole'.

3 After around ¼ mile, veer left, following the bridleway and cross the river. Proceed to the top of a gentle rise.

4 Pass through a gate on your right. Walk ahead towards the M25 and cross. Go down the steps on the left and turn right at the bottom. A few yards past the gate, bear left to enter Wisley Common. Fork left, then go straight over a junction onto a path that brings you to a road and car park.

5 Turn left for 150yd to a fork. Go right and keep ahead briefly on the concrete drive.

6 Then turn right by Oakland Lodge. If you wish to visit RHS Wisley, stay on the drive to reach the main entrance. To continue the walk, keep ahead walking between the fencing. After just under ½ mile, you reach the drive leading to a golf club.

7 Cross and continue ahead along the track to the road leading towards Ockham Mill, to the right.

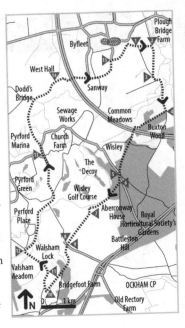

⑧ Having admired the buildings and the cascading water, return to the road for about 100yd.

⑨ Take the footpath on the right. On entering woodland, cross the bridge and go straight ahead emerging onto a common. Keep ahead to a roadway.

⑩ The walk continues by turning right. The village of Ripley is to the left with various refreshment options. Walk along the roadway, and having passed all the buildings.

⑪ Go left along a lane. Just past Millstream Cottage and River End Cottage, walk along the path to reach the Wey and the Navigation at Walsham Gates. Cross.

⑫ Turn right past the cottage and continue along the towpath. After a mile, Pyrford Lock and The Anchor Inn are reached.

⑬ Stay on the towpath as far as the second bridge opposite West Hall Care Home.

⑭ Turn away from the canal passing through a metal barrier. Follow a lane over the M25 and on to St Mary's church. Keep ahead along this residential road to the junction with Hart Road.

⑮ Turn right to return to the start.

Points of interest

RHS Wisley – George Fergusson Wilson purchased the site in 1878. He established the Oakwood Experimental Garden, with the idea of making 'difficult plants grow successfully'. Acquired in 1903 by the RHS its educational and scientific roles were enhanced when a small laboratory was opened and the School of Horticulture founded.

Hydon's Ball and Enton

START At SU954414, Milford Station

DISTANCE 7 miles (11.25km)

SUMMARY Moderate walking, occasionally hilly but generally easy underfoot

PARKING At the station or there is limited space on the roadside nearby

MAPS OS Sheets Landranger 186; Explorer 133 and 145

WHERE TO EAT AND DRINK The Merry Harriers, Hambledon, www.merryharriers.com

Plenty of opportunity to see pretty cottages and picturesque lakes in this charming area of Surrey.

① Turn left over the level crossing and immediately left along a roadway parallel to the railway.

② Continue ahead past a house and after 75yd cross a stream (WP2) and proceed uphill. Skirt the new housing development to reach a road.

③ Turn left downhill and continue to a sharp left bend.

④ About 50yd past this, take the footpath up right. Walk alongside the lake.

⑤ Turn right at a wall. Follow the path as it climbs and passes fields on the left and right. Continue to meet a track and pass houses to a road.

⑥ Cross onto a drive and veer left after 100yd onto a gently ascending bridleway meeting a road at the entrance to nurseries.

⑦ Turn right, passing the Hydon Hill Cheshire Home. At a road junction, cross over onto a track and pass the 'Hydon's Ball' wooden sign and car park on the left.

⑧ After 300yd, keep ahead at the cairn and a further 350yd, look for a right turn with a large green metal box on its path.

⑨ Go right here, passing the box, and climb up to the top of Hydon's Ball at 586ft.

⑩ Descend on the path to the left of the triangulation pillar, dropping down and curving around to the left to meet a track by a NT sign. Turn right to pass the Thames Water Booster Station on your left, go through a gate and across fields to reach St Peter's Church, Hambledon.

⑪ Beyond the church, by the wall of Stable Cottage, take the right footpath.

⑫ Dropping down to The Merry Harriers, take the bridleway along its right side, to a two-plank bridge.

⑬ Just beyond the bridge, fork right. Walk ahead following the line of poles.

⑭ Turn right at a crossing path to go through woods and emerge into a field.

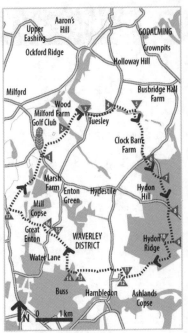

Pass a lake and after 200yd go left to climb a field. At the brow of the hill, go into the next field and walk down, half-left to a stile by a holly hedge.

⑮ Cross the stile onto a path and follow it to a road. Go straight across to Great Enton.

⑯ Beyond the converted barn, turn left. Pass under the railway to the charming cottages and continue along the lane to a large brick building.

⑰ Here, turn right immediately along a footpath and keep ahead for ¾ mile to arrive back at Milford Station.

Points of interest

Hydon's Ball – One of the highest points in Surrey, it is a memorial to National Trust co-founder Octavia Hill.

Weybridge and Walton-on-Thames

START At TQ068647, Town Lock KT13 8XX

DISTANCE 7 miles (11km)

SUMMARY An easy riverside walk

PARKING Free street parking can be found nearby

MAPS OS Sheets Landranger 187; Explorer 160

WHERE TO EAT AND DRINK The Queen's Head, www.whitebrasserie.com/locations/weybridge.html. Open daily 11:00–23:00; Sundays 12:00–22:00

The Minnow, www.theminnow.co.uk. Open daily 11:00–23:00; Thursday to Saturday til midnight; Sunday til 22:30

The Anglers, www.anglerswalton.com. Open daily 11:00–23:00; Friday and Saturday til midnight; Sunday til 22:30

A pleasant walk along the rivers Wey and Thames with a glimpse of a 14th century manor house.

① To begin this walk, cross both bridges and immediately turn right onto the towpath beside the River Wey. In just over ½ mile, Thames Lock is reached.

② Cross the bridge, and go along the cinder track with green railings on your left. Join a drive and after around 80yd, turn right to cross a green and cream bridge.

③ Turn left along Church Walk, continuing through the barriers and passing cottages.

④ At The Old Crown, turn left along Thames Street, walking to the bend at the start of Walton Lane. Go through a parking area. The route soon reaches the steps, the starting point for the foot ferry to Shepperton.

⑤ Next, the route reaches the bridge across to the private D'Oyly Carte Island, beyond which is the start of the Desborough Channel. The return route will bring you down the steps of the bridge but for now pass underneath both this, and the similar bridge at the other end of the channel, about 2/3 mile away. The path curls round through the Cowey Sale parking area and then passes under Walton Bridge.

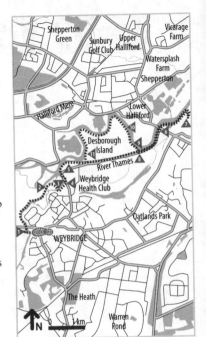

⑥ Having gone over the blue plank bridge beyond Walton Marina, the walk reaches the moorings at Walton Wharf and also river frontage of The Anglers pub. Turn right, and right again at the top to catch a glimpse of the Grade 1 listed Old Manor House.

⑦ Retrace the route to the bridge at this end of the channel, and go up the steps, turning right over the water.

⑧ Follow the road down to the bend.

⑨ Keep ahead along the drive signposted for 'Weybridge Vandals' rugby club.

⑩ When the drive bears left, continue ahead on the narrow path, following the course of the river. Immediately after a mini beach, fork left to join a road.

⑪ Cross the bridge that bears a panel commemorating the opening of the Desborough Channel in 1935. Descend the steps to reach the outward route, turn right and retrace your steps to return to the start.

Points of interest

D'Oyly Carte Island – Richard D'Oyly Carte, the producer of the Gilbert and Sullivan comic operas, acquired the island, previously known as Folly Eyot, in 1890.

Holmwood and Coldharbour

START At TQ169472, St John's Church, North Holmwood RH5 4JH

DISTANCE 7¼ miles (11.5km)

SUMMARY Moderate walking

PARKING Plenty available on the road

MAPS OS Sheets Landranger 187; Explorer 146

WHERE TO EAT AND DRINK The Plough Inn, www.ploughinn.com. Open daily from 12:00–23:00; Sunday til 22:30. Food served 12:00–15:00; 18:30–21:00

1️⃣ From the side of the church, take the path leading away from the village and pass two log posts at the entrance into woodland. When you reach a clearing leave the gravel path and veer half right. Bear left, and then fork right after 50yd. As you exit this woodland there is a small path on your right heading down to the A24. Cross over and turn right. Go past the Red Chilli Indian restaurant and walk 50yd along the A24.

2️⃣ At the 'North Holmwood' sign, turn left and go up the steps. Go forward to cross a bridge and then head in the general direction of a line of poles, towards a red-brick house.

3️⃣ Turn left along a road for 150yd.

4️⃣ Then go right to Chadhurst Farm. Beyond the house and pond, walk ahead between the outbuildings and go through a metal gate.

5️⃣ Once over the crest of the hill beyond, you will go through a kissing gate and as you continue, and go through more gates, you will eventually reach a road.

6️⃣ Cross the road and proceed along the drive to Squires Farm. Go past the house and then go left on a path skirting the lawn to enter a forest.

7️⃣ At the top of a small incline, stay left on the bridleway.

8️⃣ At a path fork, go left through woodland to reach a gravel crossing track. Here, go ahead up a steeper section, and at the top, bear right.

⑨ Then turn left past an isolated house. Continue along this bridleway to reach Coldharbour and the Plough Inn.

⑩ Go left along the road to a junction, from where there is a fine view to Ranmore church.

⑪ Turn right by White Cottage.

⑫ At the top of a rise, turn left down a drive signposted 'Anstiebury Farm'. Keep ahead between the barns, with the farmhouse over to the right.

⑬ Stay on a grass path, ignoring the stile to the right. Your descent brings you to brick gate pillars at Taresmocks.

⑭ Go over the stile just down to the left and continue by the wall.

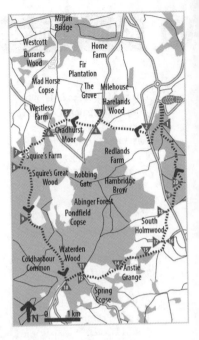

⑮ After about ¼ mile and at the bottom, leave the woodland and walk along the side of a field to exit in its right corner. Turn left along the roadway, with the tower of St Mary Magdalene ahead.

⑯ At the junction just above Betchets Green Farm, turn sharp left.

⑰ Then take the footpath to the right when you are under the trees. Cross a bridge and walk along the bottom of a field to reach a road. Walk straight ahead through Warwick Close.

⑱ Turn right beyond the barrier to cross the A24. Take the main grassy path half-left, entering Holmwood Common.

⑲ Go diagonally across some grassland and drop down onto a gravel path. Turn left and keep going until you reach signs for a viewpoint.

⑳ At the viewpoint, take the slope down half-left towards the two tower blocks. This becomes a track through woodland. At a junction, follow the signs for North Holmwood to return to the start.

Ranmore Common and Polesden Lacey

START At TQ141503, Denbies Hillside car park, Ranmore Common RH5 6SR

DISTANCE ¼ miles (13.25km)

SUMMARY Moderate walking on a variety of terrain

PARKING National Trust Pay and Display car park at the start

MAPS OS Sheets Landranger 187; Explorer 146

WHERE TO EAT AND DRINK Polesden Lacey, www.nationaltrust.org.uk/polesden-lacey. Lovely café serving great cakes and sandwiches, and roasts on Sundays. Open daily 1:00–17:00

A walk around Ranmore Common and along the North Downs Way with an opportunity for a detour to Polesden Lacy.

1 Walk away from the church as far as the last house on the right, with the two prominent chimney stacks, and take the track signposted to the Youth Hostel. Once past the hostel, continue along the track, climbing up and ignoring a track off to the right. Pass under a bridge and continue for about ¾ mile to reach an approach road.

2 Turn left to reach a fork signposted towards several cottages including 'Prospect Lodge', keep following signposts for the cottages.

3 Beyond the house at the crest, pass under a thatched bridge, and at the end of the sloping wall, continue ahead down a yew-lined embankment.

4 At a path junction, bear right up to Yew Tree Farm. Continue on the main track for a further 200yd to reach a gate on the right.

5 Go through into a field and cross it keeping to the top side. In the second field, descend diagonally to a gate, turn left up the track beyond.

6 Go past Pigden Cottage and walk on to reach another house, Hogden Cottage.

7 Just beyond this, turn up right onto a track. Cross the road and

continue along the track. Descend on a holly-fringed path to join the drive leading from Haneys. Cross the road, taking the drive into Friars Elm for 100yd. At a bend, go over the stile and cross two fields then descend to a road.

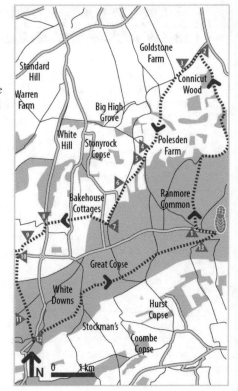

⑧ Cross the road slightly to the right and take the path which climbs the bank, bearing left and staying parallel to the road. Go through the kissing gate out of the woodland and bear left around the field. Keep ahead, following the telegraph poles and go over the stile by the green metal gate.

⑨ Diagonally cross the next field, heading towards the buildings, then take the path between the buildings, up the drive to reach the road by a sign for 'Dunley Hill Court'.

⑩ Cross the road and take the path past Red Gables. Go ahead at the path crossing. Keep ahead at another crossing. Shortly the path reaches a T-junction where you turn right to reach the reservoir.

⑪ Turn left immediately before the railings to emerge from the woodland. Keep left and go down the trail with a dip to the left. Soon you will reach a second dip on your right; follow the path round clockwise to descend onto the North Downs Way.

⑫ Turn left to reach a road. Cross and keep on the North Downs Way for about two miles.

⑬ When you finally emerge from the woodland, cross the grassy slope diagonally to the left to reach the car park and the start of the walk.

100 Bookham and Effingham Commons

Start At TQ128556, Bookham station KT23 3JG

Parking Free side-street parking is available by the station

Distance 8½ miles (13.75km)

Maps OS Sheets Landranger 187; Explorer 146

Summary Easy level walking across commons, through woodland and passing lakes

Where to eat and drink The Bakery, www.thebakeryshop.co.uk. Closed Sundays

An interesting walk including areas with substantial houses, crossing commons, through woodland and passing lakes.

1 Leaving Bookham station, turn left along the road to the bend. Go to the far end of the Tunnel Car Park to an NT information board and contribution pillar. Take the bridleway to the left, which runs straight through woodland and is signposted to Handley's Cottage and Merritts Cottage. After just under ½ mile pass a pond on the right and arrive at Merritts Cottage. Shortly, take the left public bridleway to 'Effingham Common'.

2 Cross a stream on a concrete bridge and at the junction turn right and continue to follow the public bridleway and blue arrow passing houses on your left.

3 Fork left then go right onto a footpath marked with a yellow arrow. Go directly across the field ahead to reach another stile and bridge. Go straight across the field through a gate. At the end of the next field, aim for the railway arch in the distance. Beyond this, a track leads to a road.

4 Go across to a path that goes through woodland with a large cleared area on the left. Follow the yellow arrow straight ahead.

5 At the wide track turn left to pass commercial buildings on your right. Follow to reach a road. Turn right.

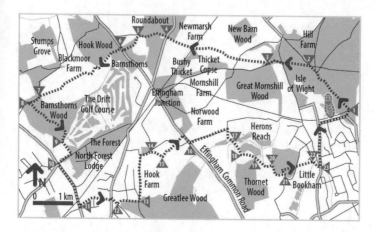

6 Then very soon cross and take the public footpath with a signpost to 'Lake House'. When the drive veers left, cross the stile ahead. Go over a bridge and enter a field. Keeping to the right, walk through a series of fields.

7 Keep going to reach a woodland track. Turn left and continue around 200yd.

8 Turn up left at a marker post. The path eventually descends through rhododendrons to a field boundary.

9 Go left to reach a road and turn right to reach a junction.

10 Here, go left and after the railway bridge, walk up Horsley station approach.

11 At the 'Thornleas Place' roadsign, turn right onto the surfaced footpath. Walk up to a green. Keep ahead along the road to reach a gate at the far end. Cross slightly left into Norrels Drive.

12 Turn left after 100yd, near the lodges with their tall twin chimneys. The path soon joins a road; follow it to its end, then continue along a path.

13 Cross Heath View and walk down the left side of the field. Swing right at the bottom, skirting the woodland.

⑭ Cross over a ditch using the wooden plank bridge. Follow alongside the ditch keeping it to your right. In the corner at the end of the hedgerow, keep ahead for 50yd.

⑮ Turn left along a stony track. Go past a red brick house and cricket pitch to the main road, opposite Norwood Farm entrance. Turn right.

⑯ Then turn left along Lower Farm Road. At its end, cross a metal stile and turn right to drop down to the lake.

⑰ Cross over the lake. Cross the drive and enter a field; go diagonally towards the wire fence bordering the water. Follow the fence.

⑱ At the corner of the lake go left into a field using the squeezer stile. Cross the field.

⑲ After another squeezer turn right and head away from the lake. Go diagonally to the corner and through another squeezer. Keep straight ahead crossing another field with two squeezers.

⑳ The path turns right and swings left around a thicket to reach a wide S-bend.

㉑ Here take the left path and after 250yd, go over a stile and down the left side of the field beyond to reach a residential road.

㉒ Follow the road round to the right to join the main road.

㉓ Turn left here to return to Bookham station.

Points of interest

The Bookhams – Great and Little Bookham – are part of the Saxon settlement of Bocham, 'the village by the beeches'. They are surrounded by common land. Whilst once two distinct villages, the Bookhams have long been interconnected with residential roads that give most newcomers the impression that it is in fact one large village. Polesden Lacey is a National Trust-owned regency villa on the southern edge of the village, open to the public.